Pysanky

Easter Egg Coloring Book

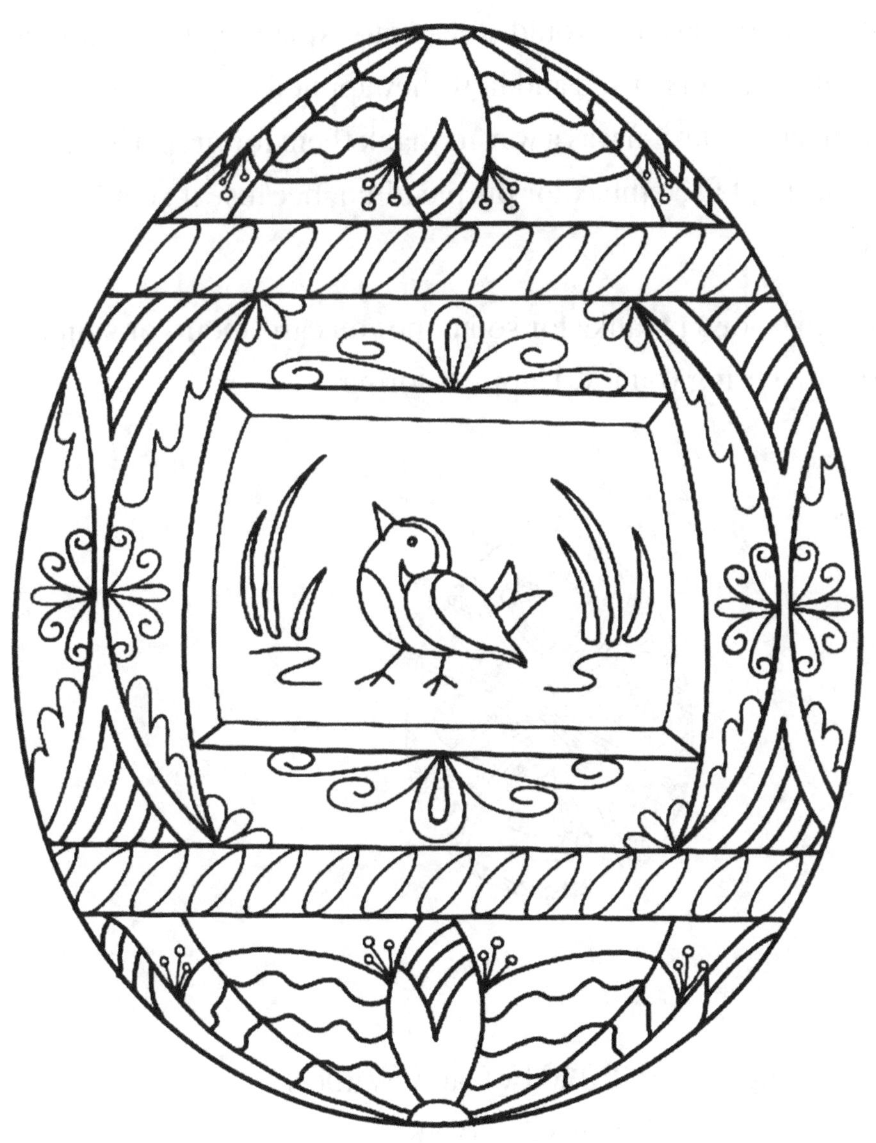

Cathy Witbeck

Calico Barn Books

This collection of pysanky images to color was designed with a mixture of traditional and non-traditional subjects in a variety of settings. I added a guide for the meanings of symbols and colors, on the inner cover, to add an extra layer of meaning to your coloring experience.

When my children were little, I used to make a pysanka for each of their teachers before Easter. I would add a note explaining the meaning of the colors and symbols I used and how they applied to that teacher. An egg with an acorn design was a way to thank them for preparing my child for the future. I used the color purple often, because it stands for patience.

Use this book to color a pysanka for someone you care about, or simply choose colors that bring you joy. Happy coloring.

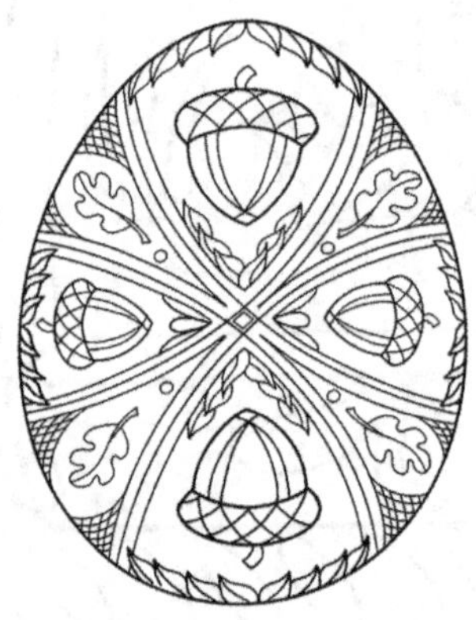

Copyright@2020 by Cathy Witbeck

ISBN: 978-1-7322626-3-8

Printed and bound in the United States of America February 2020

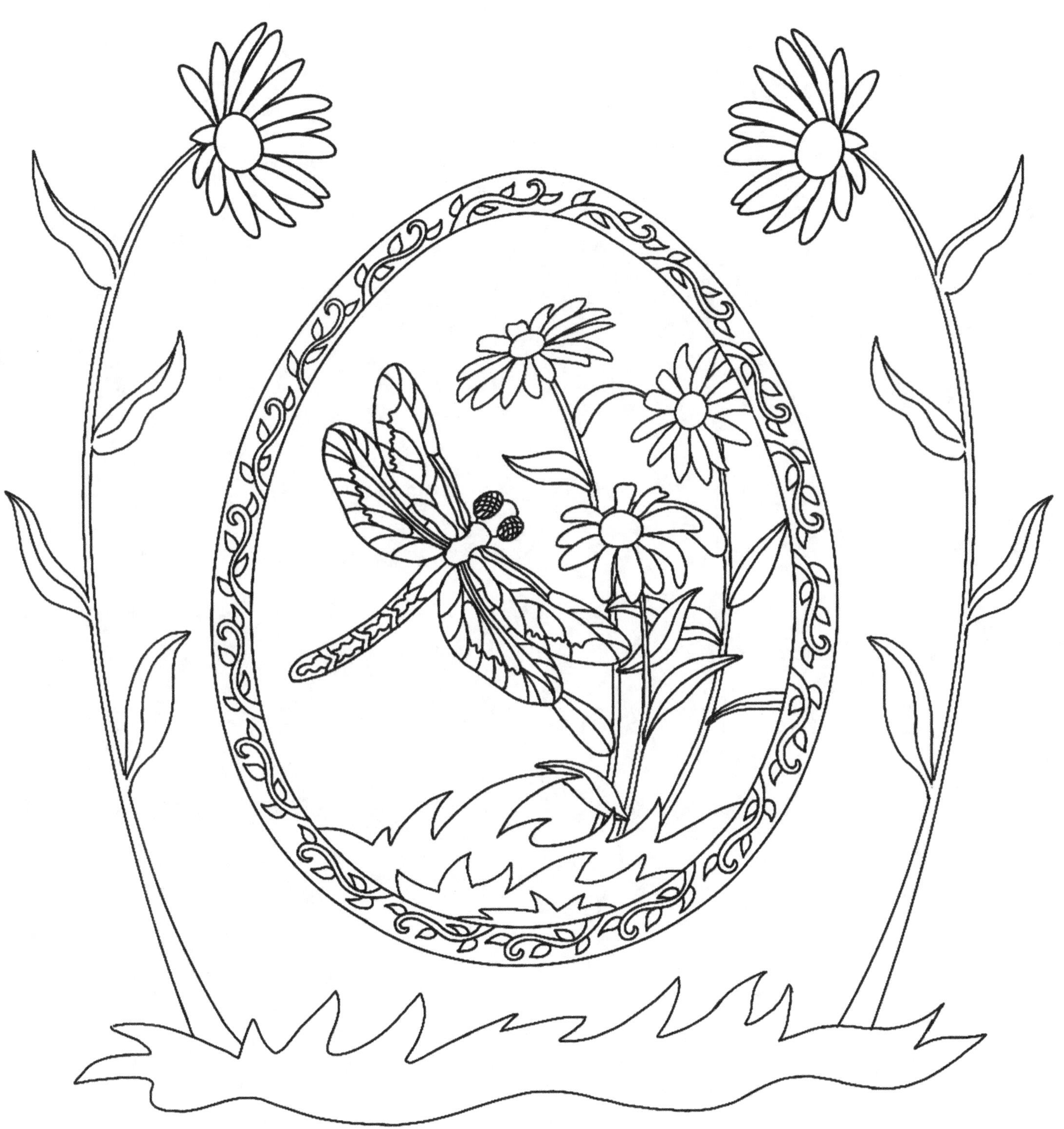

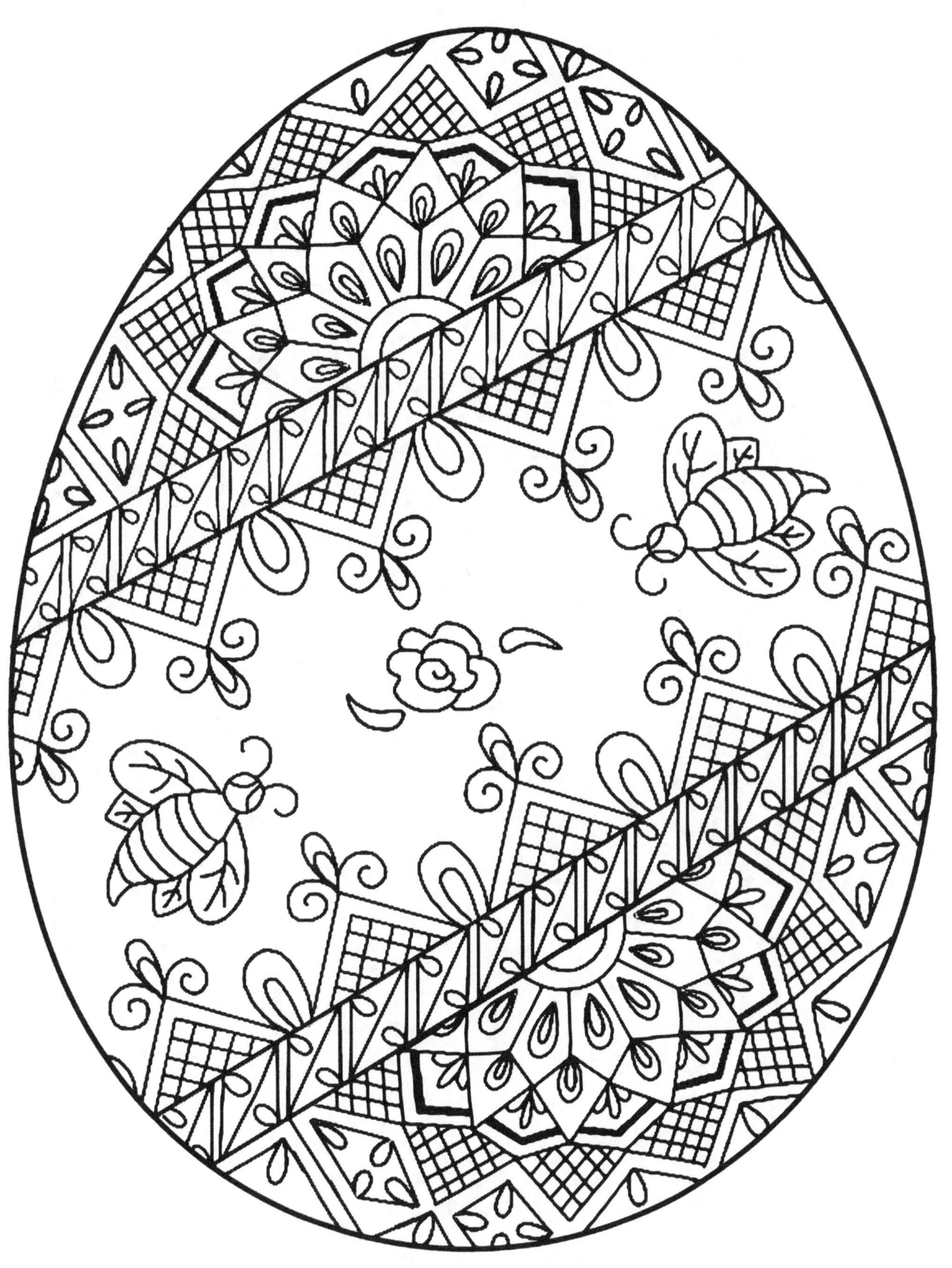

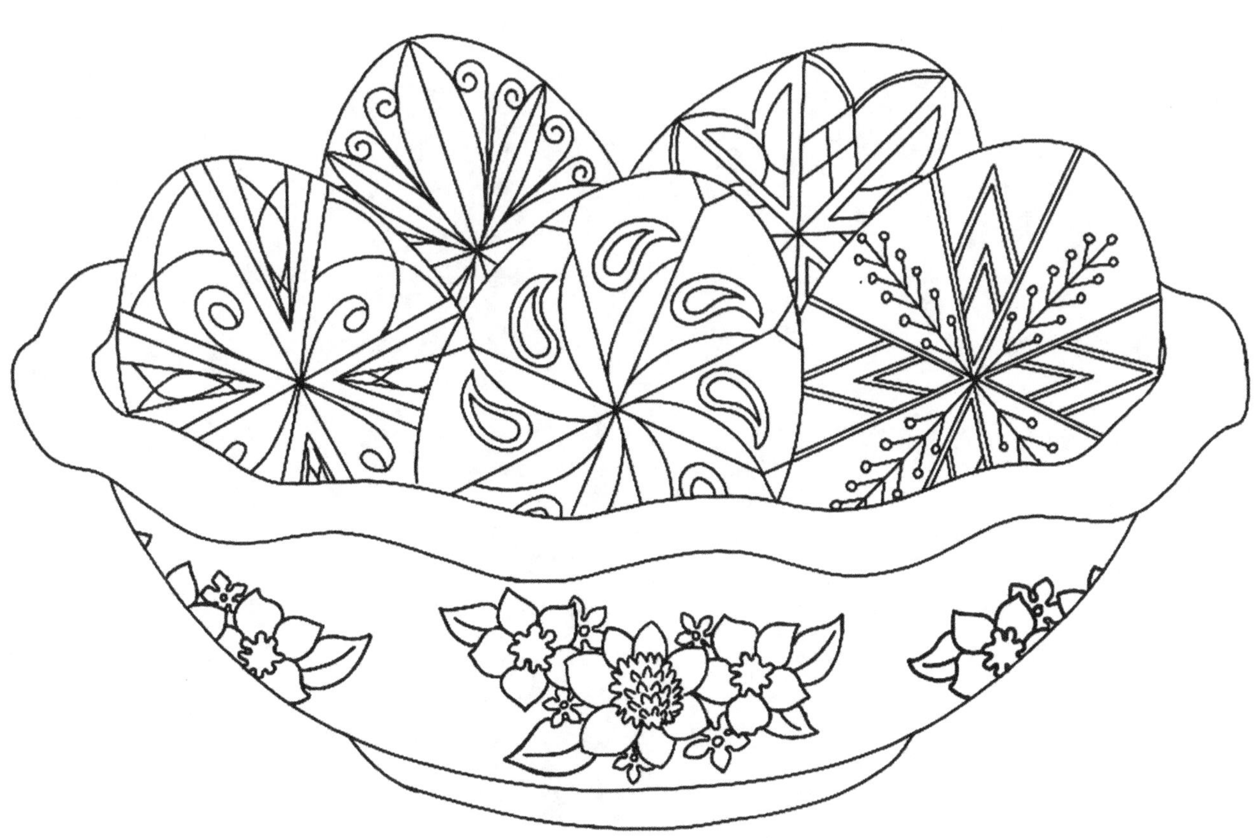

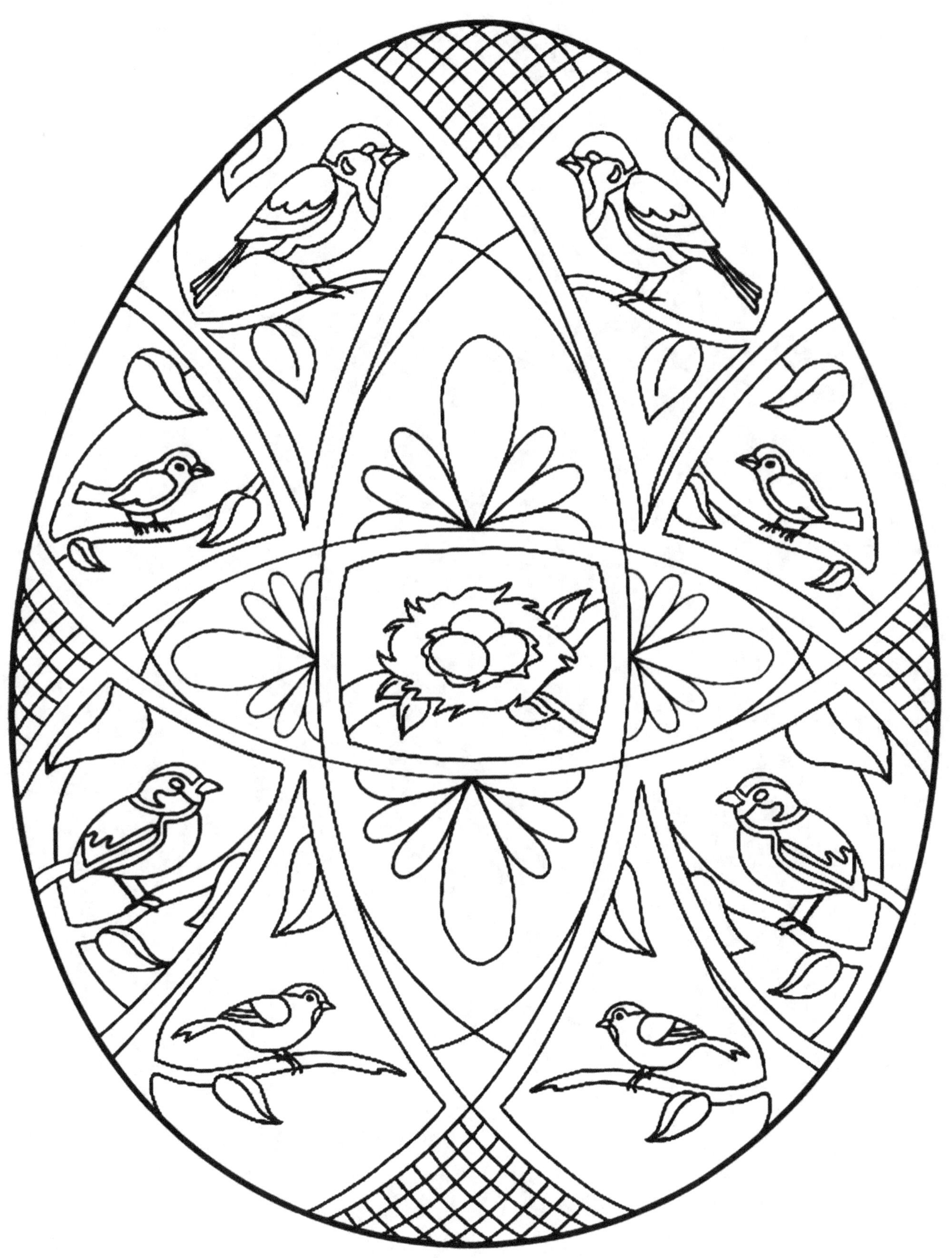

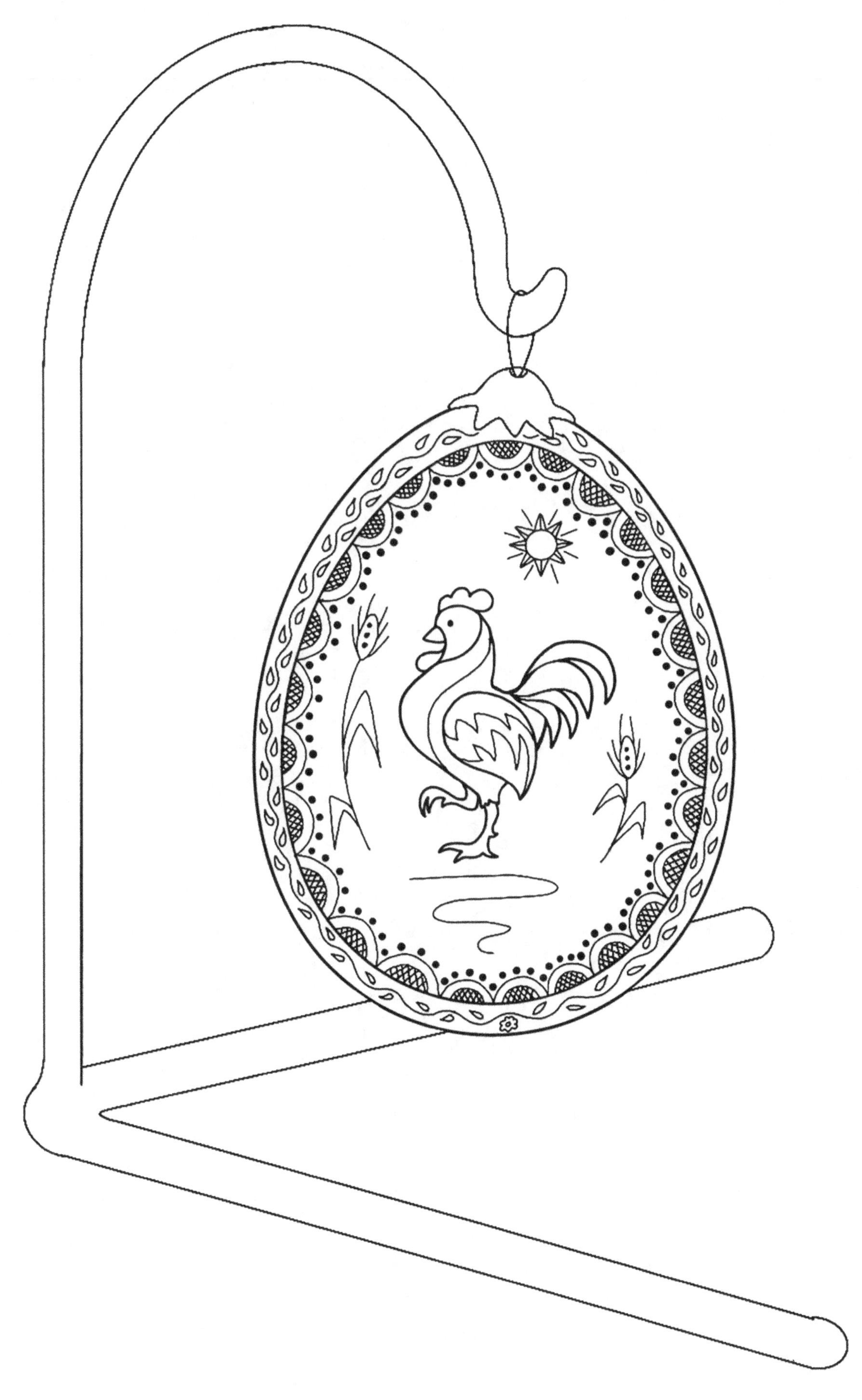

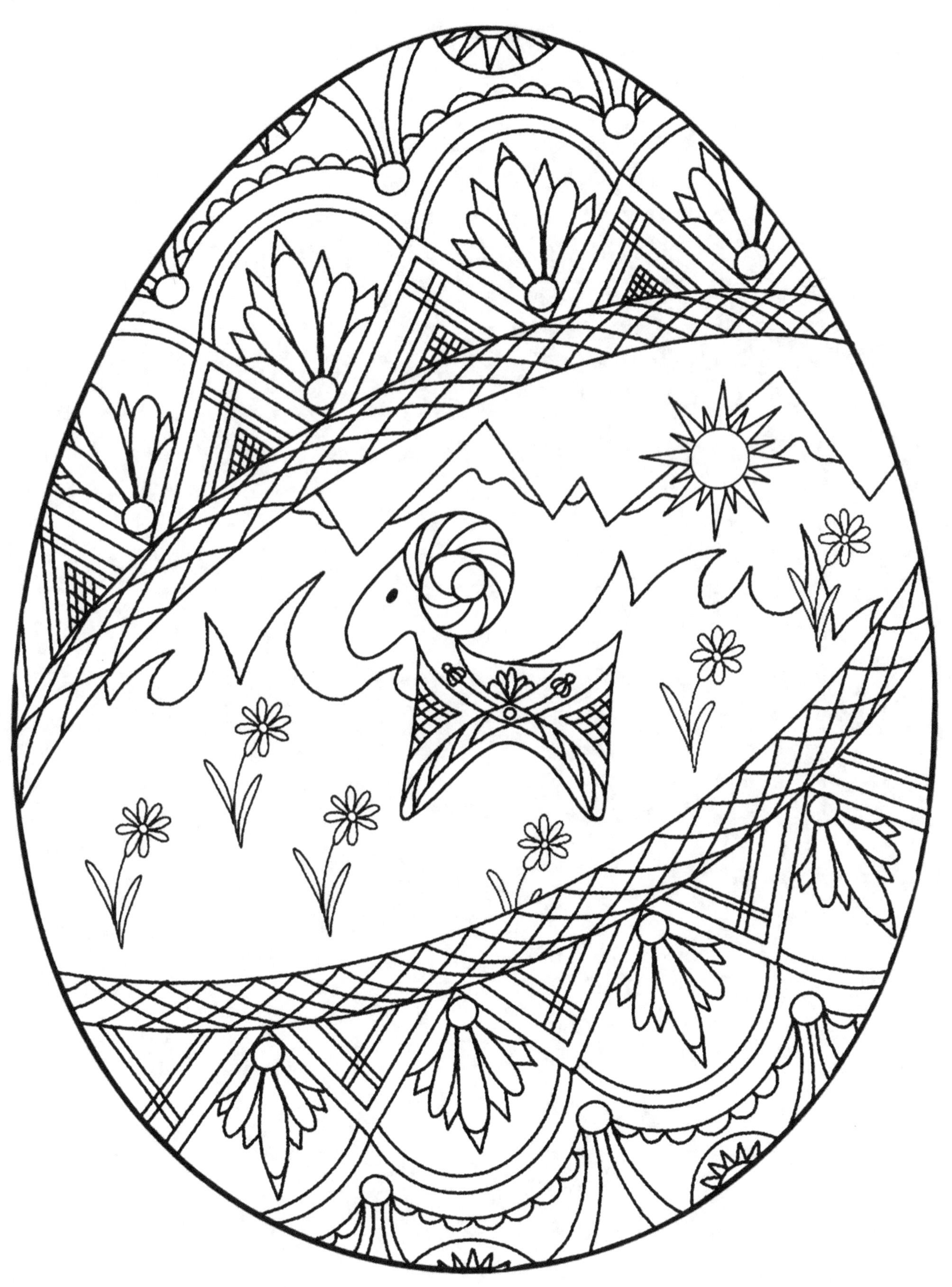

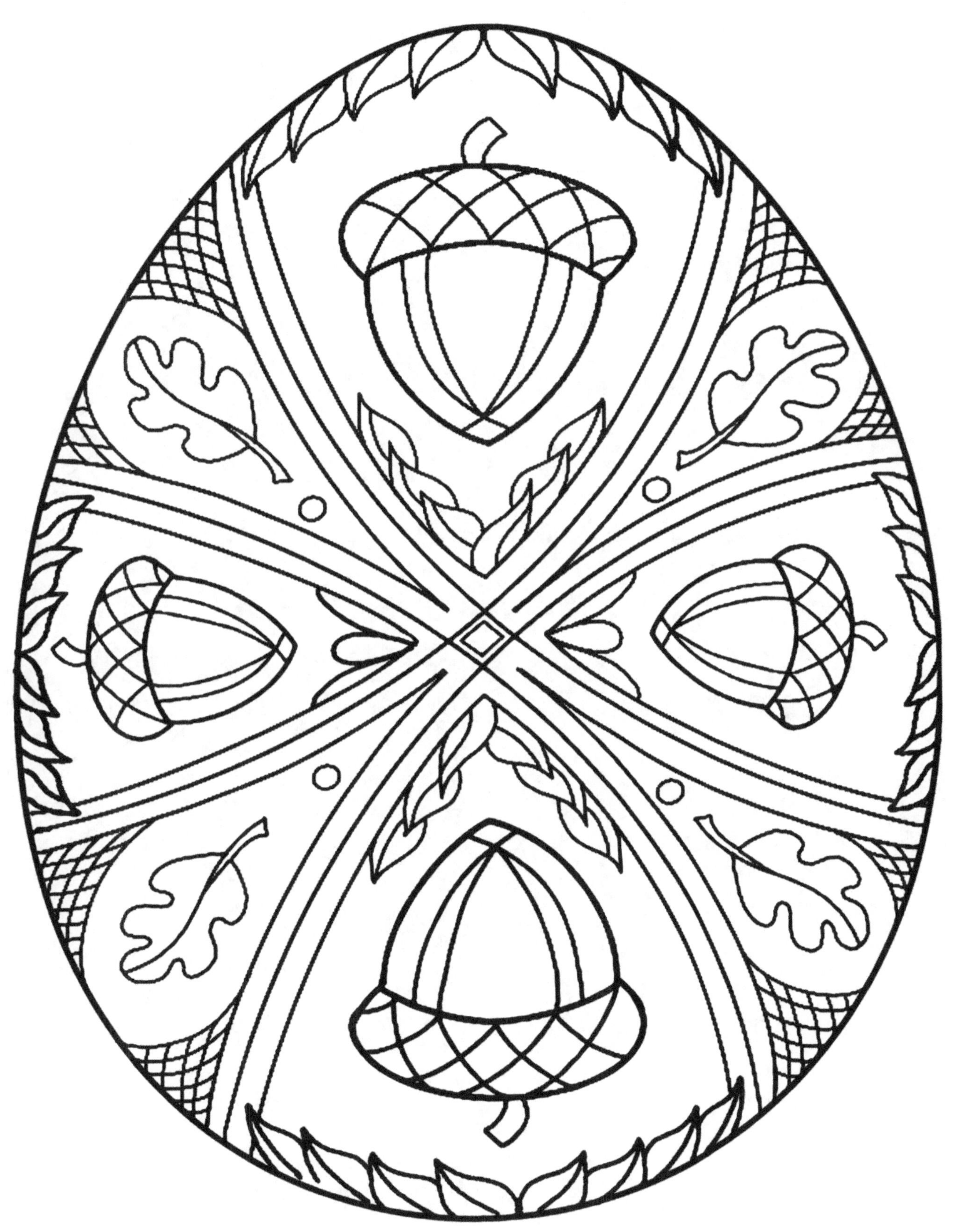

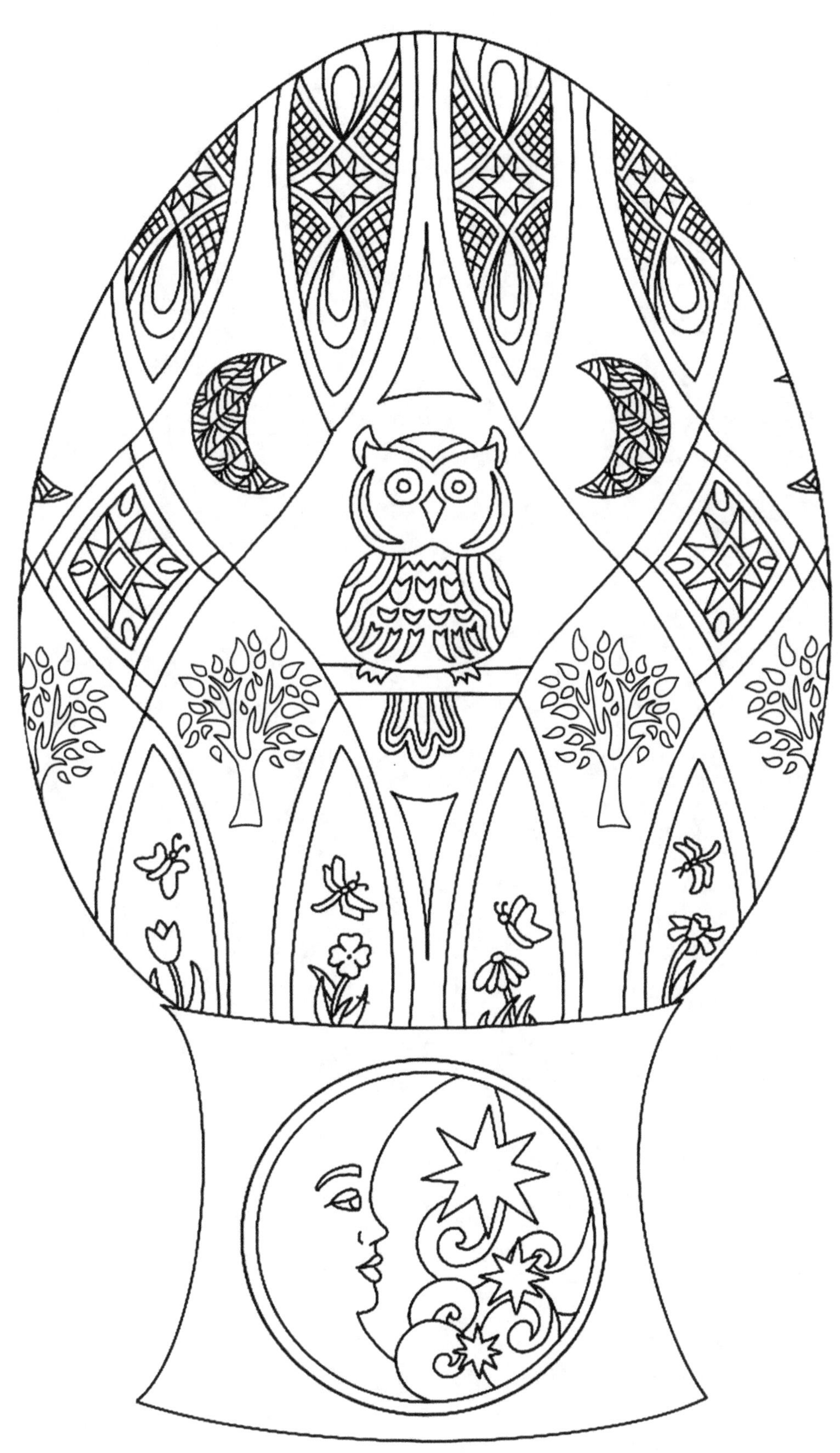

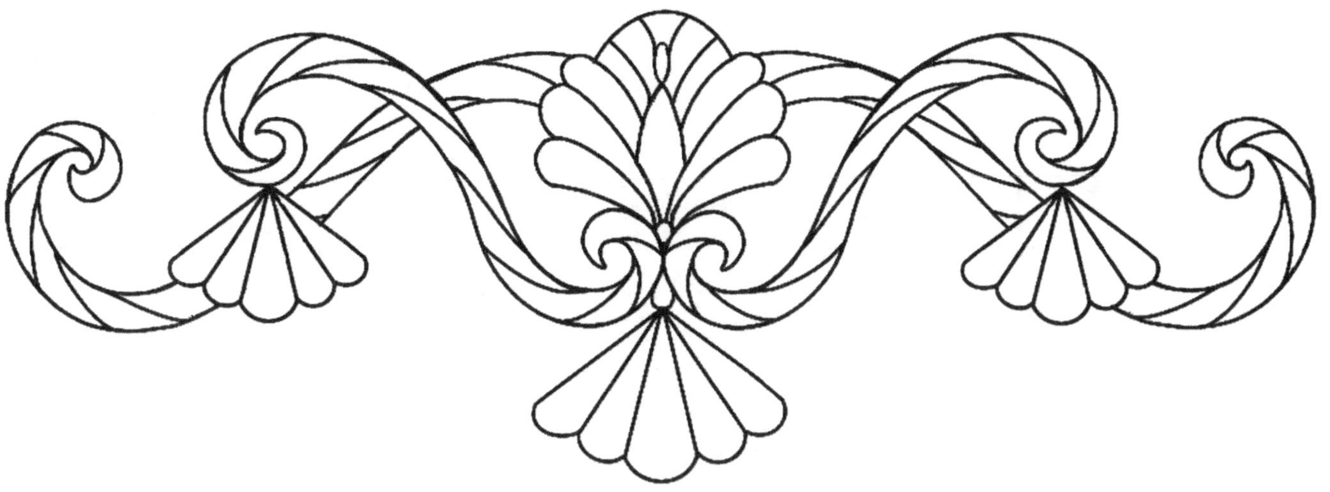

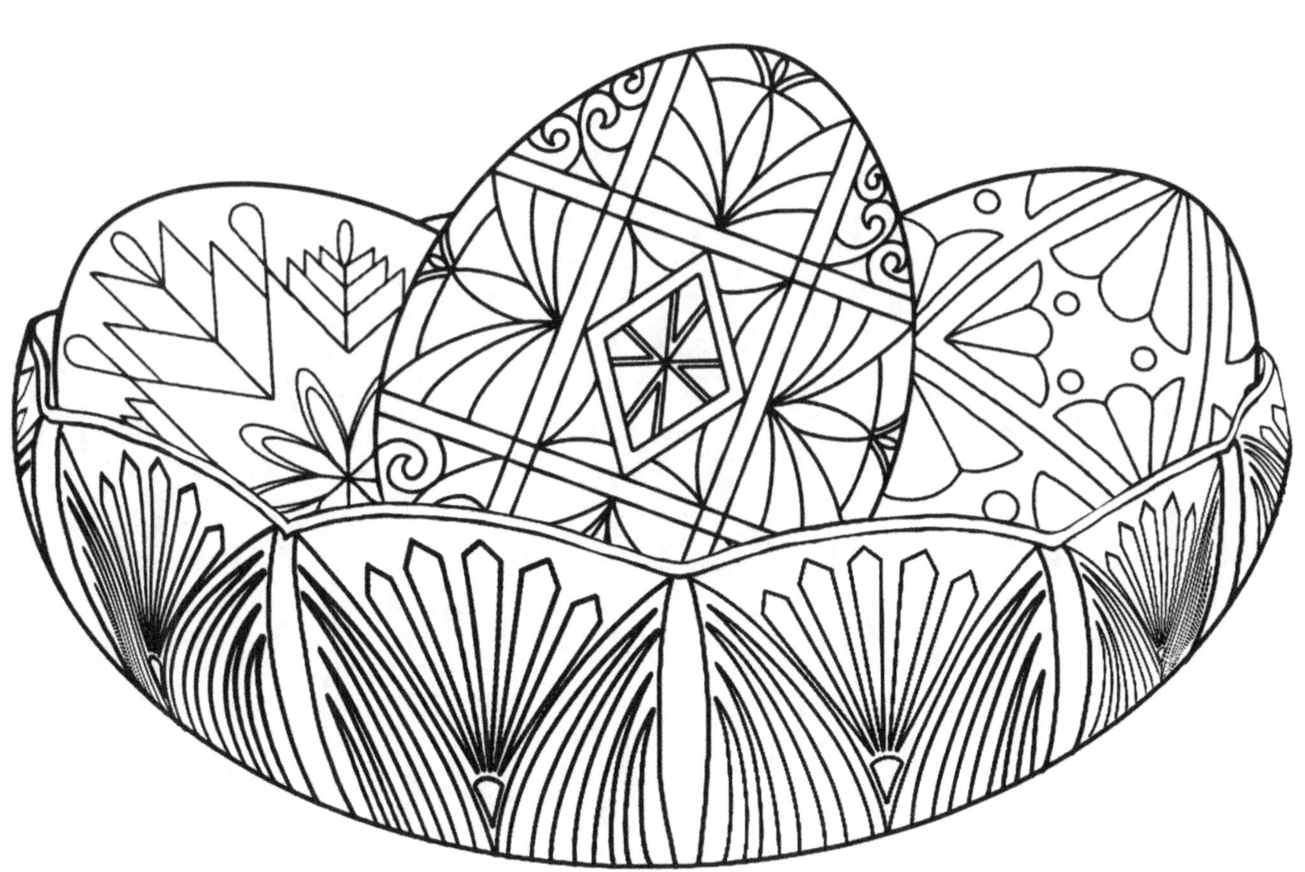

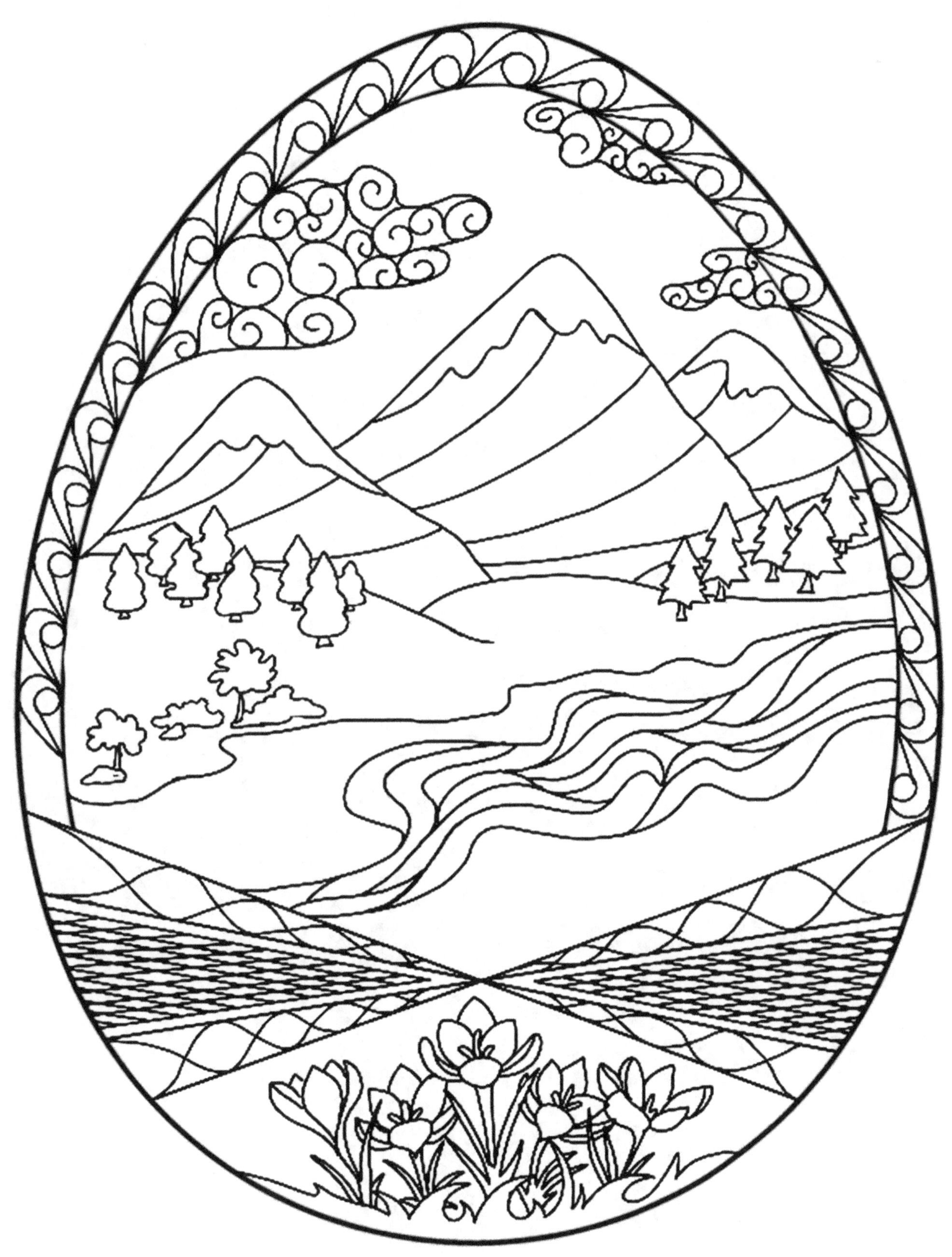

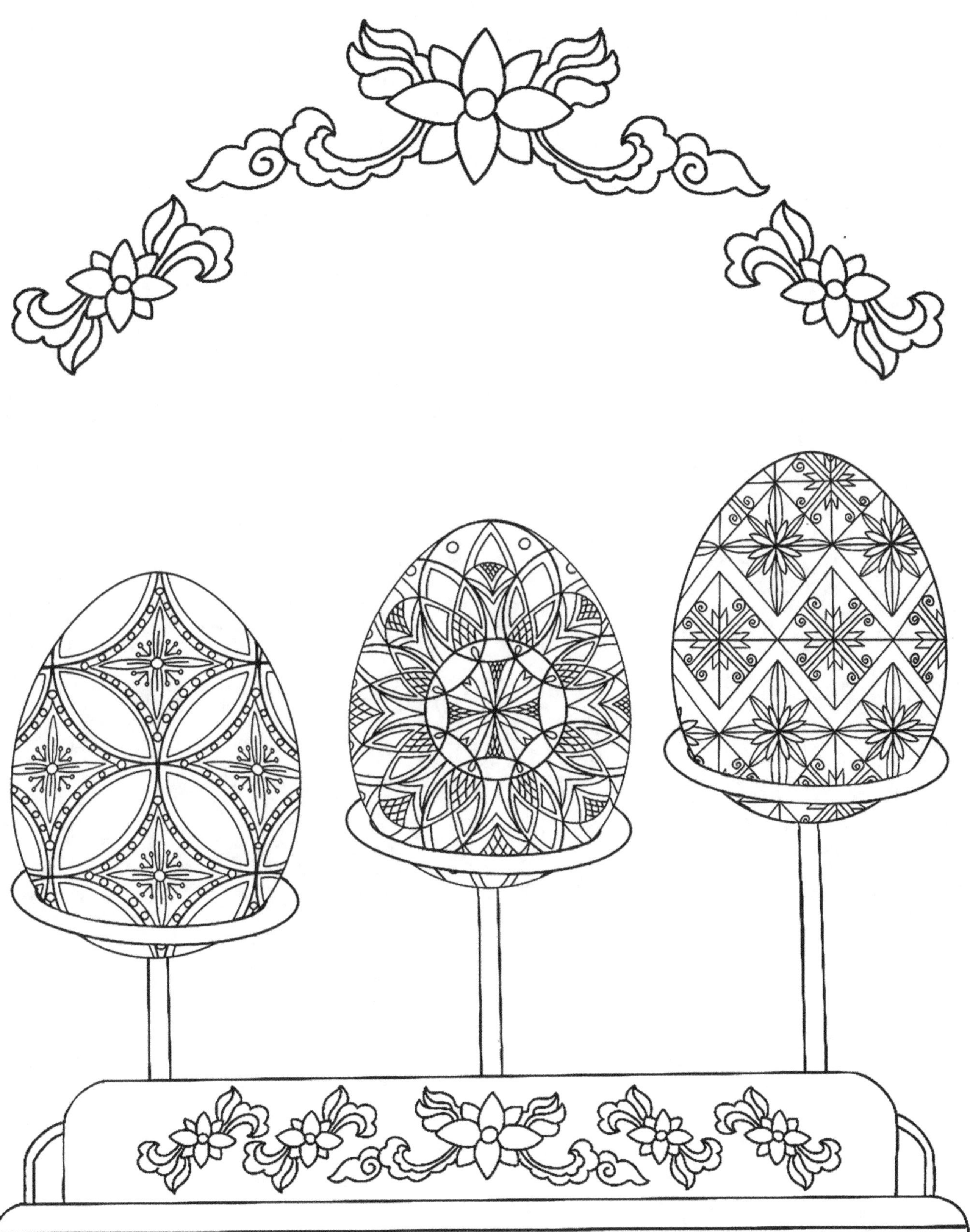

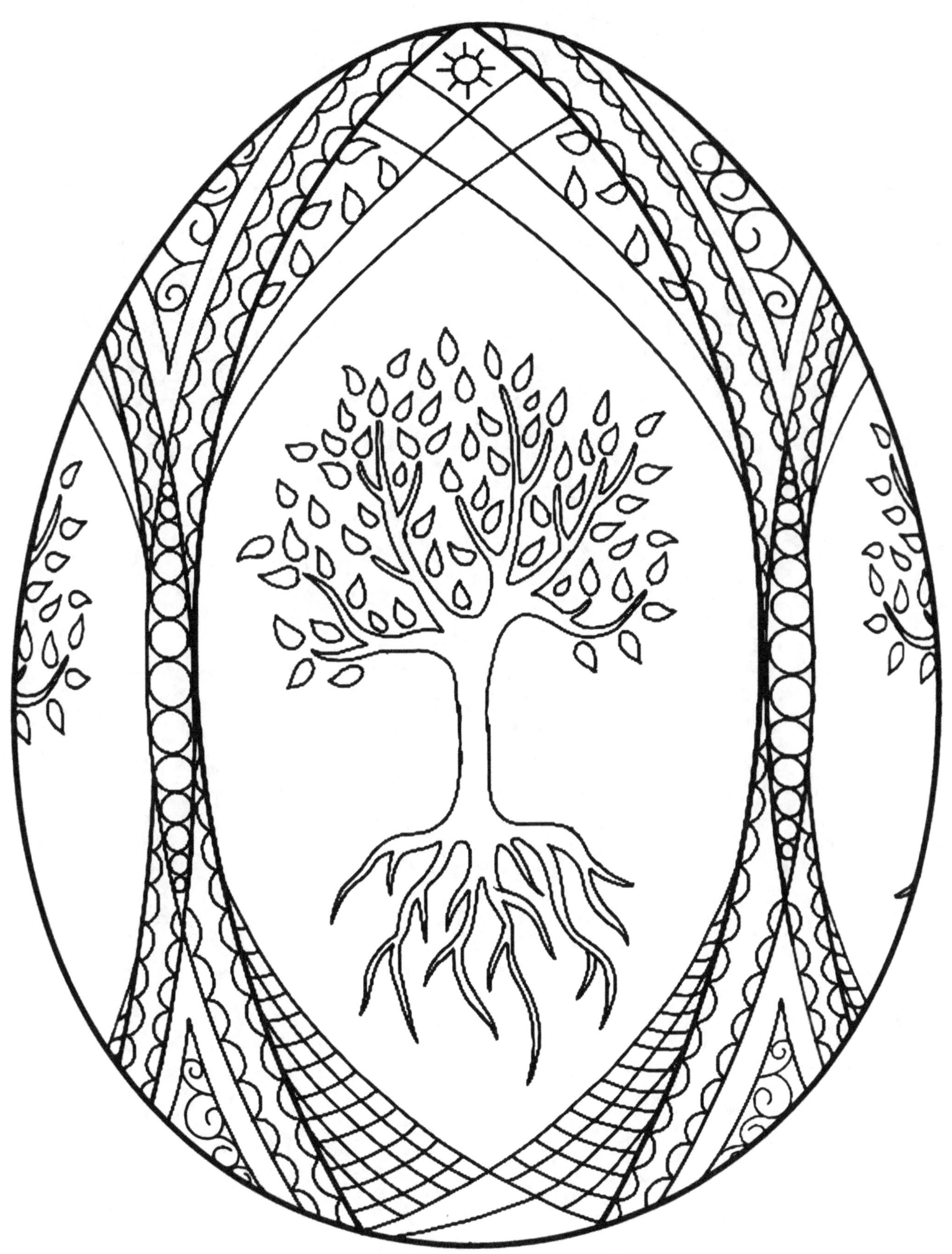

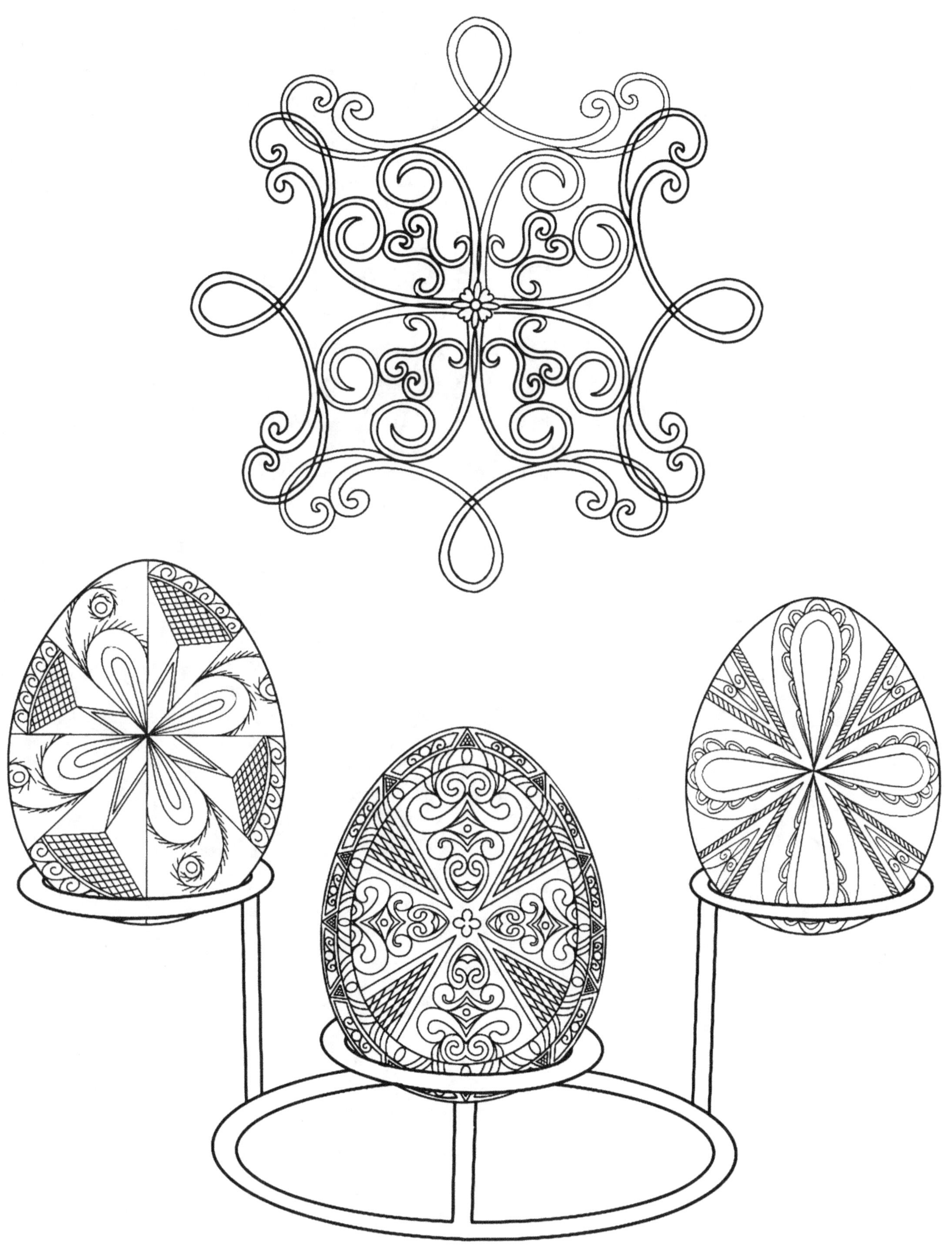

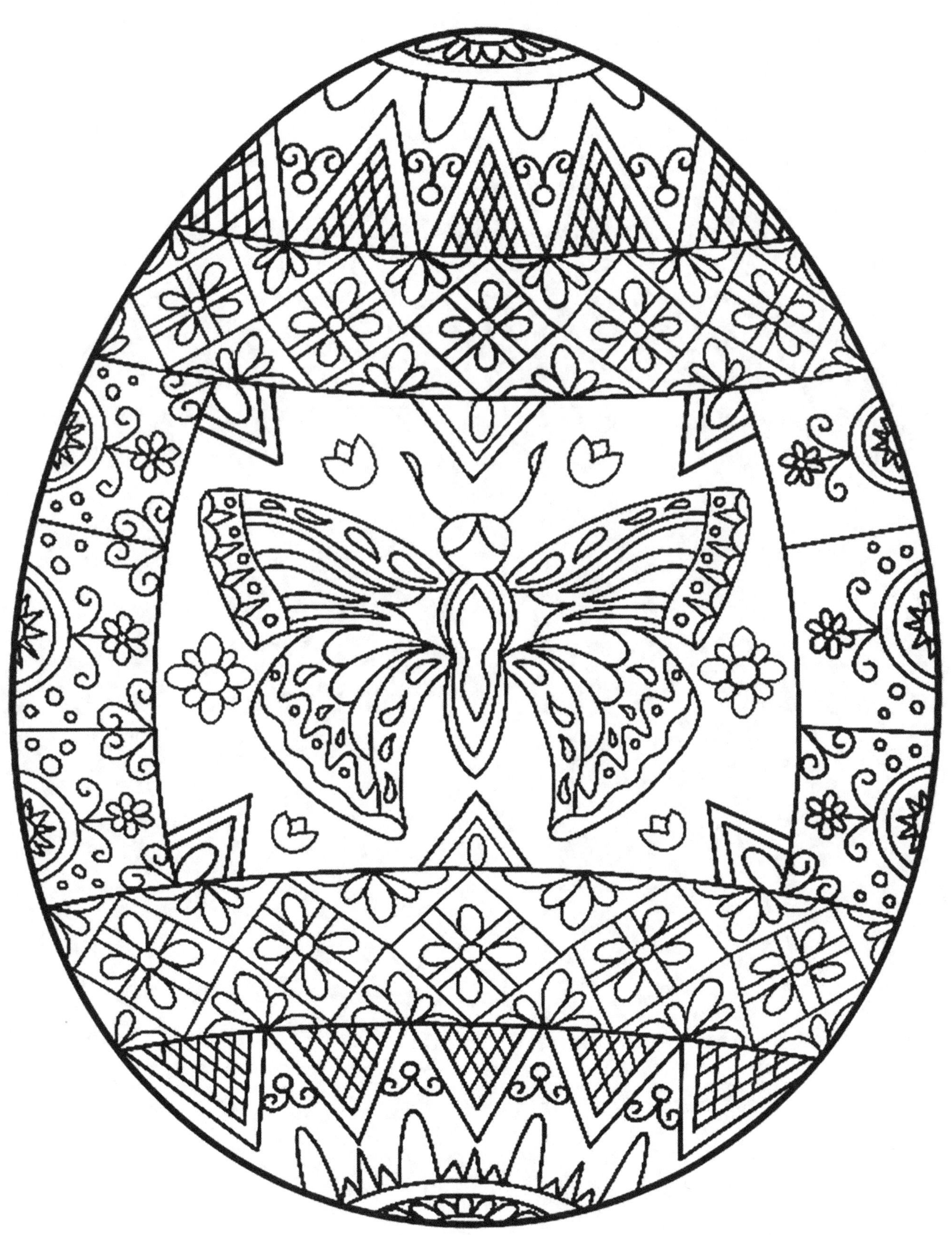

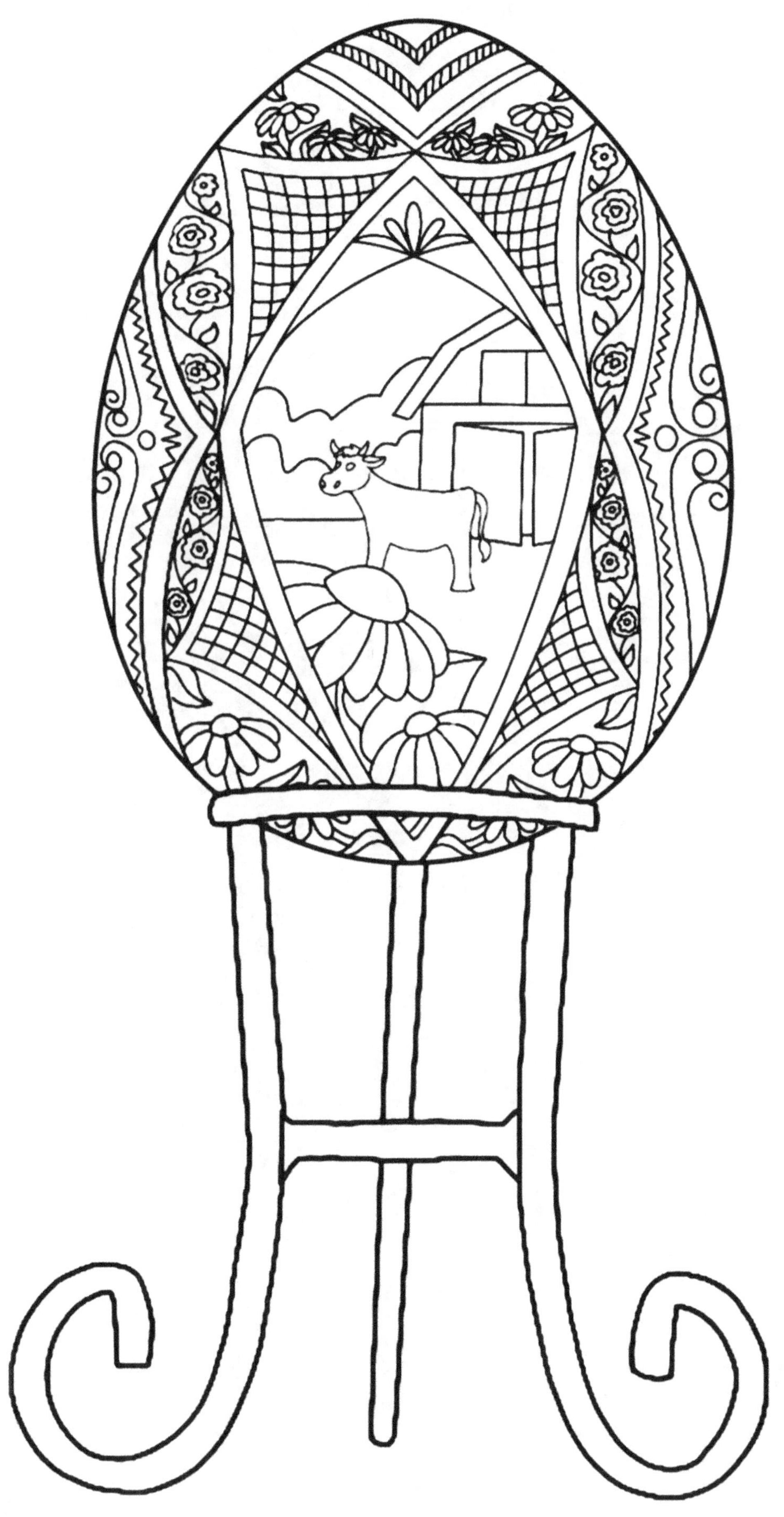

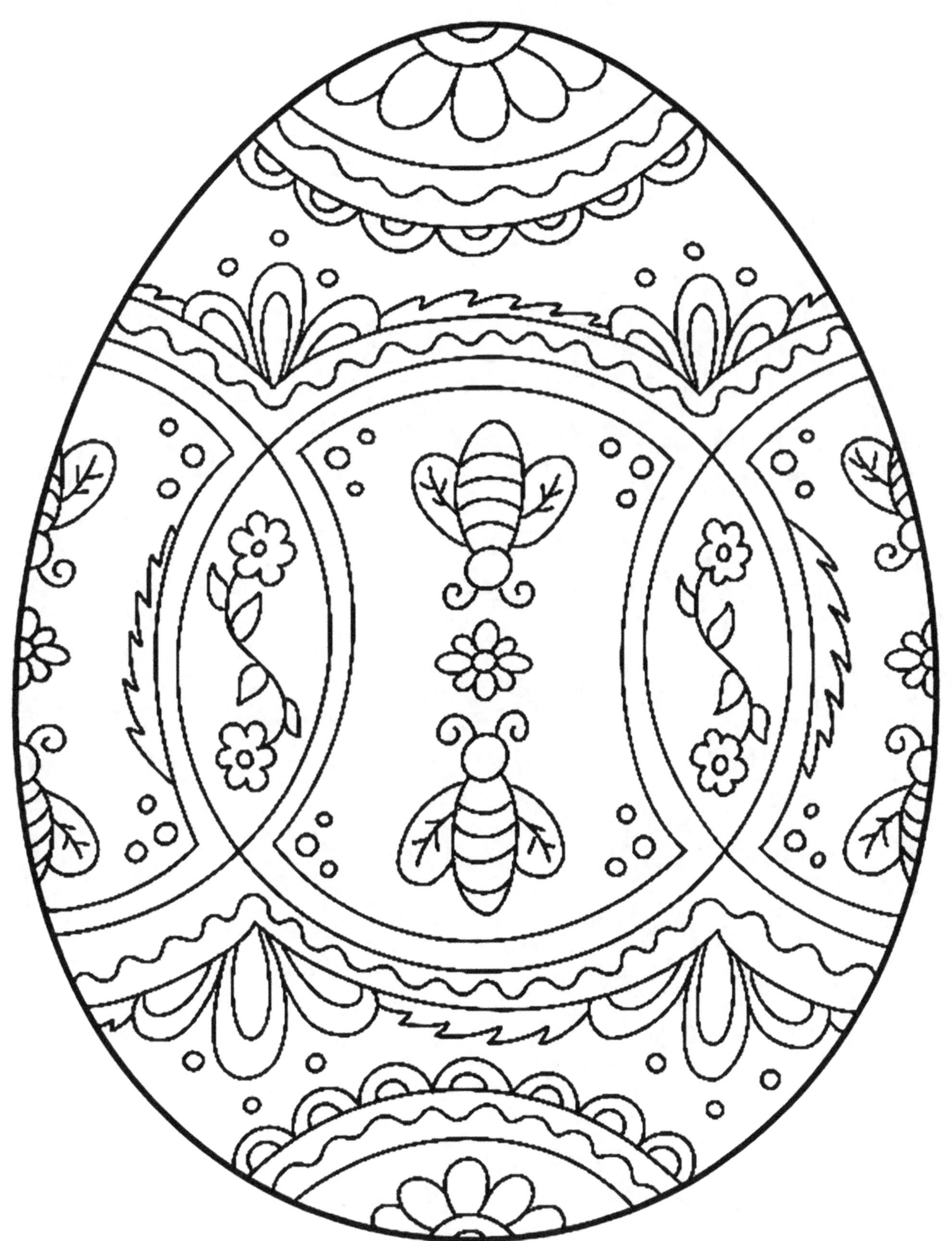

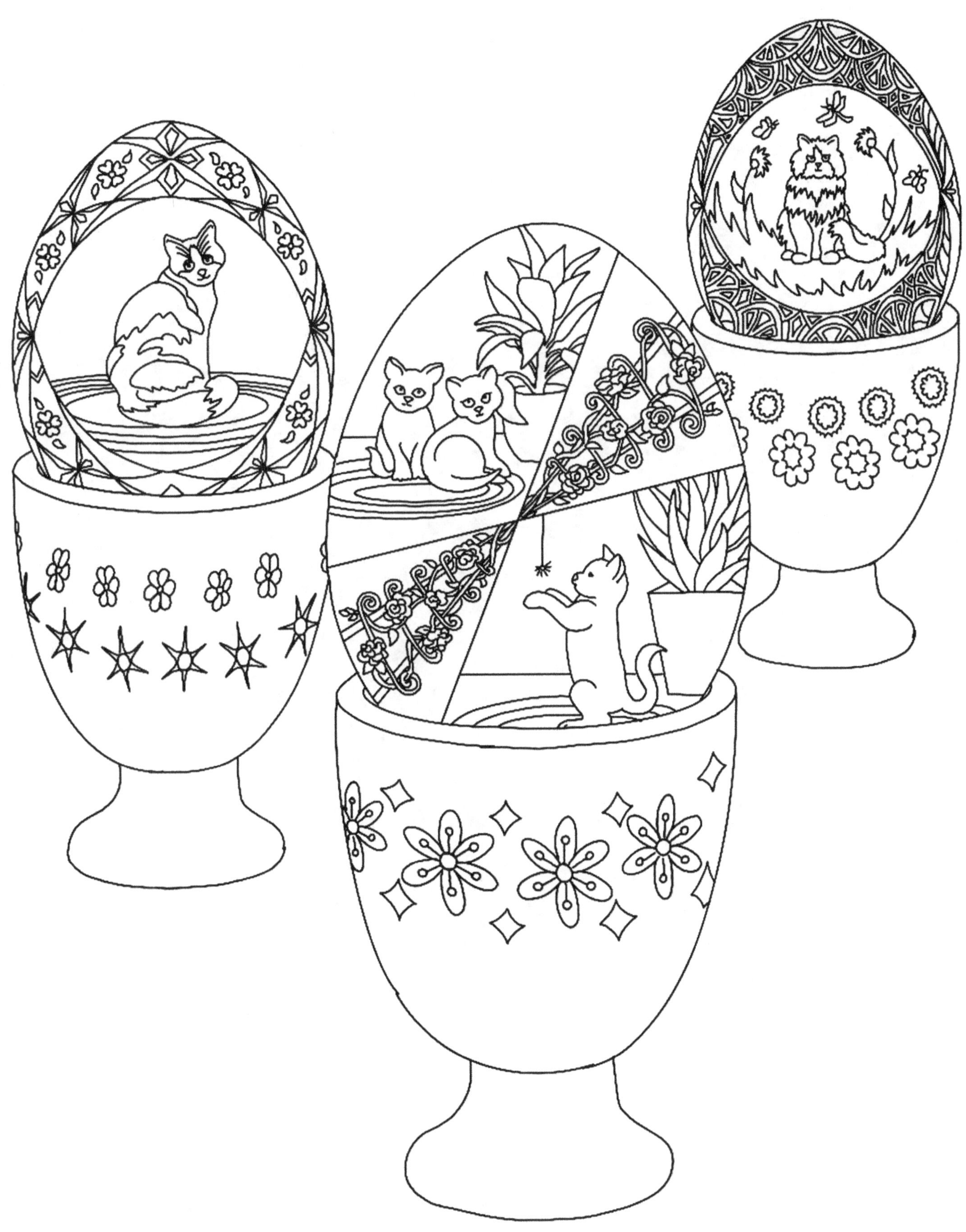

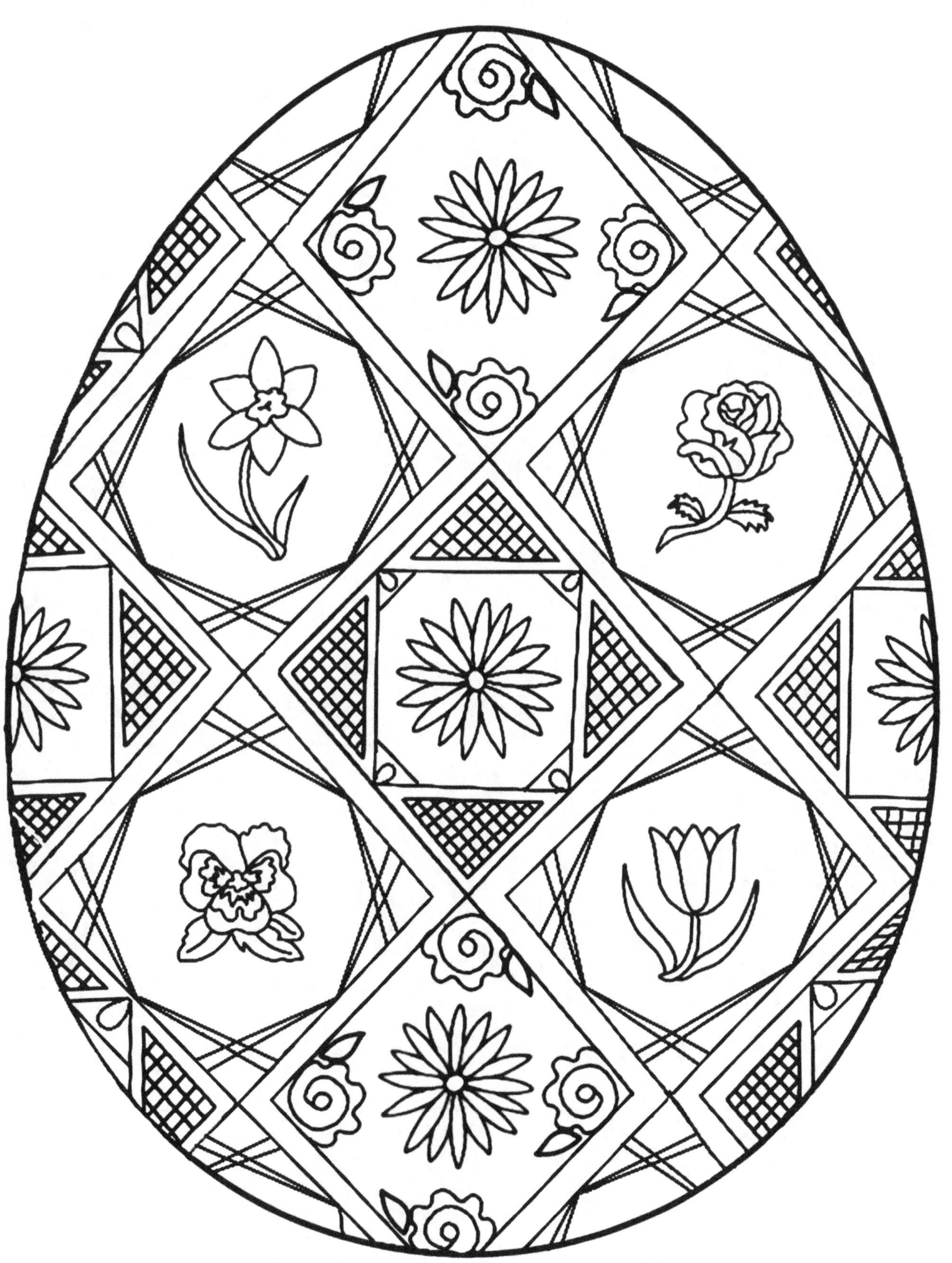

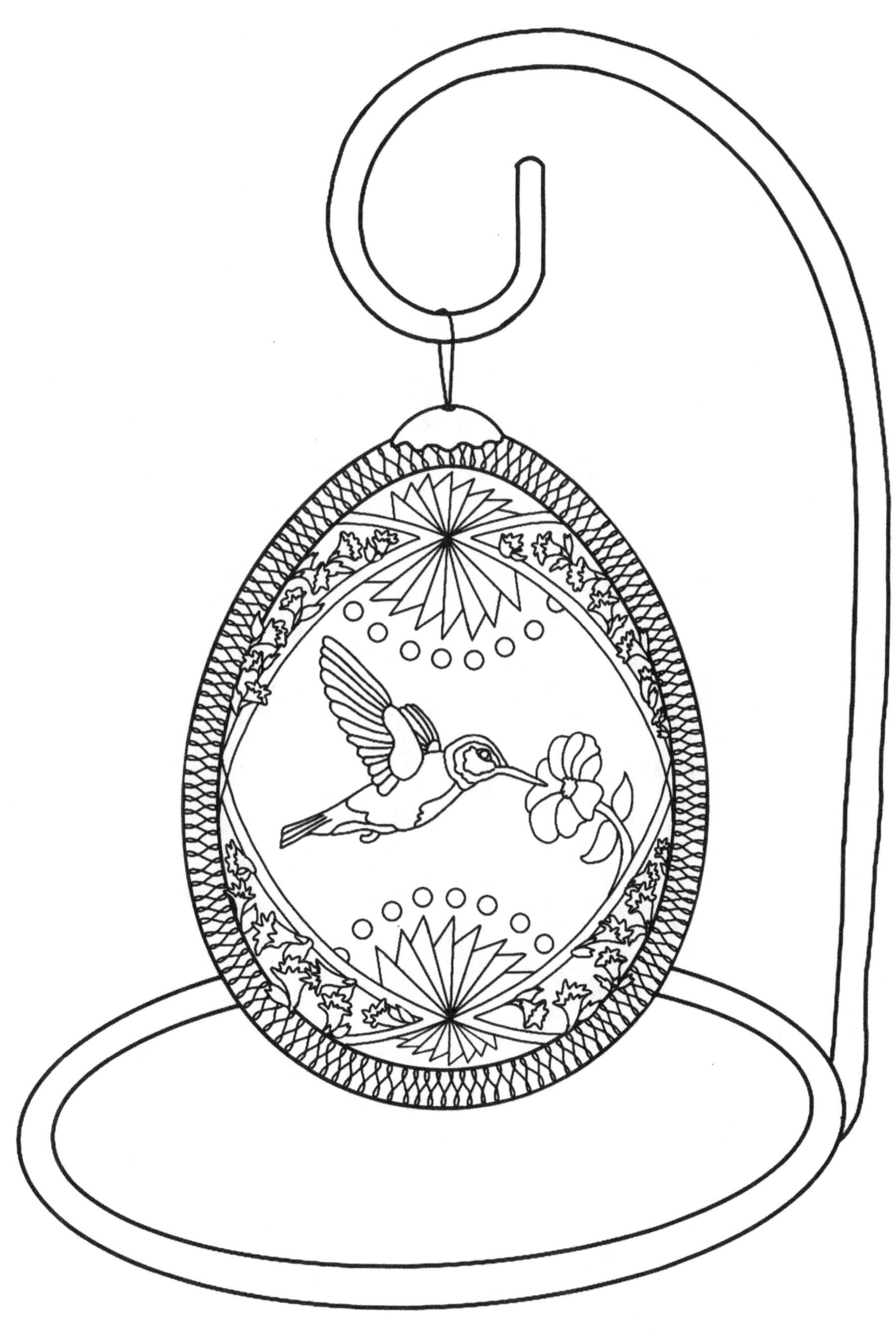

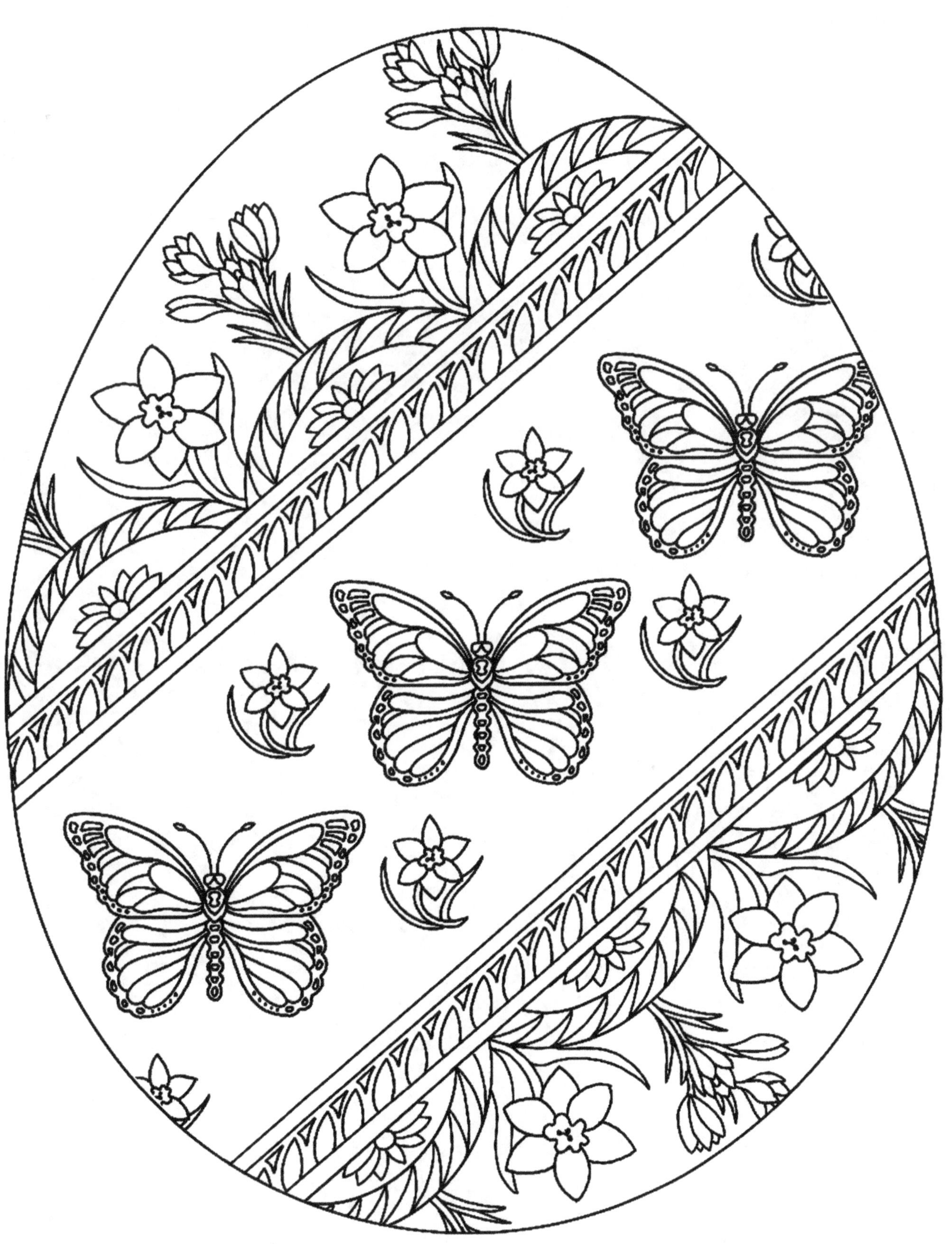

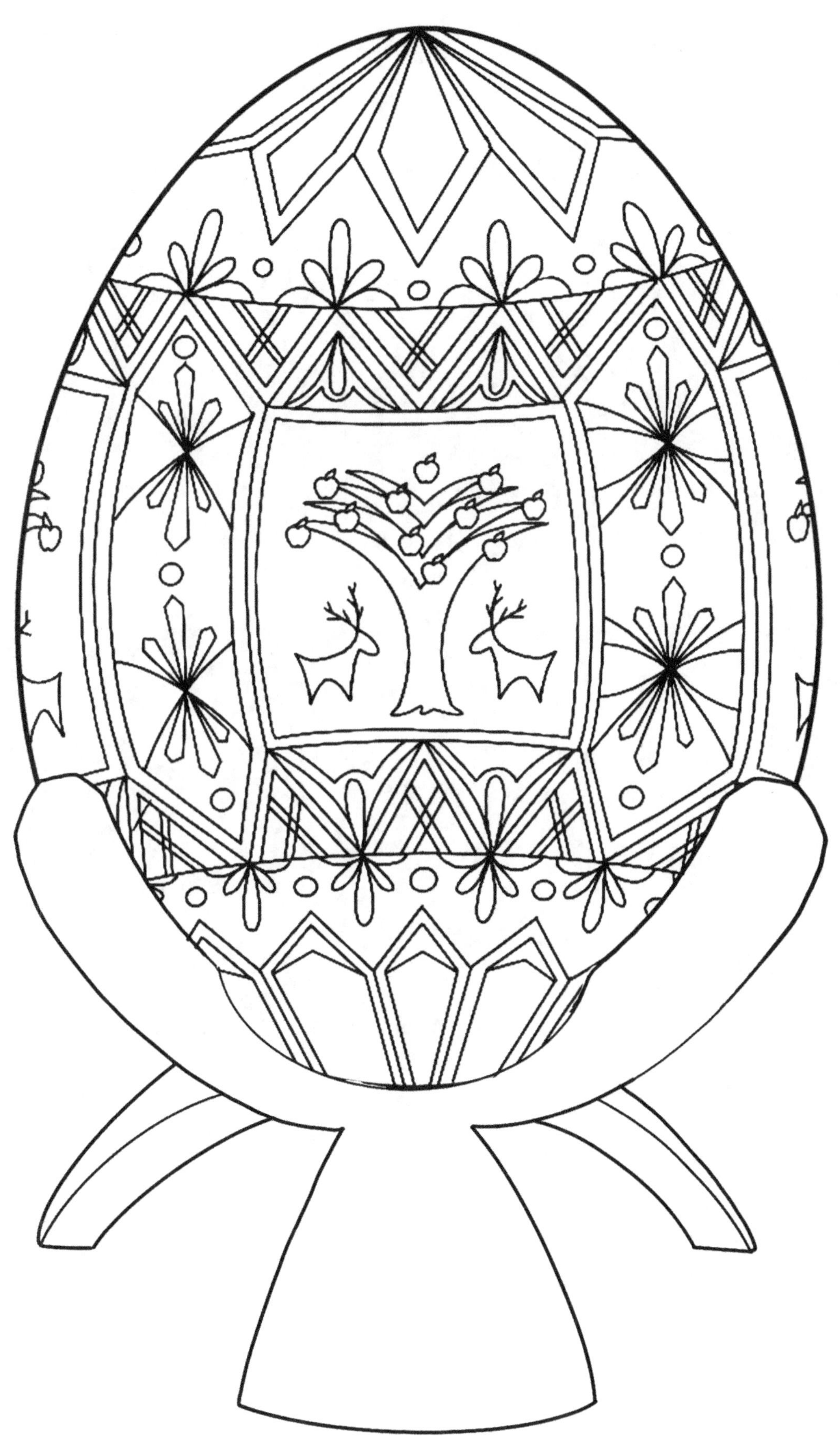

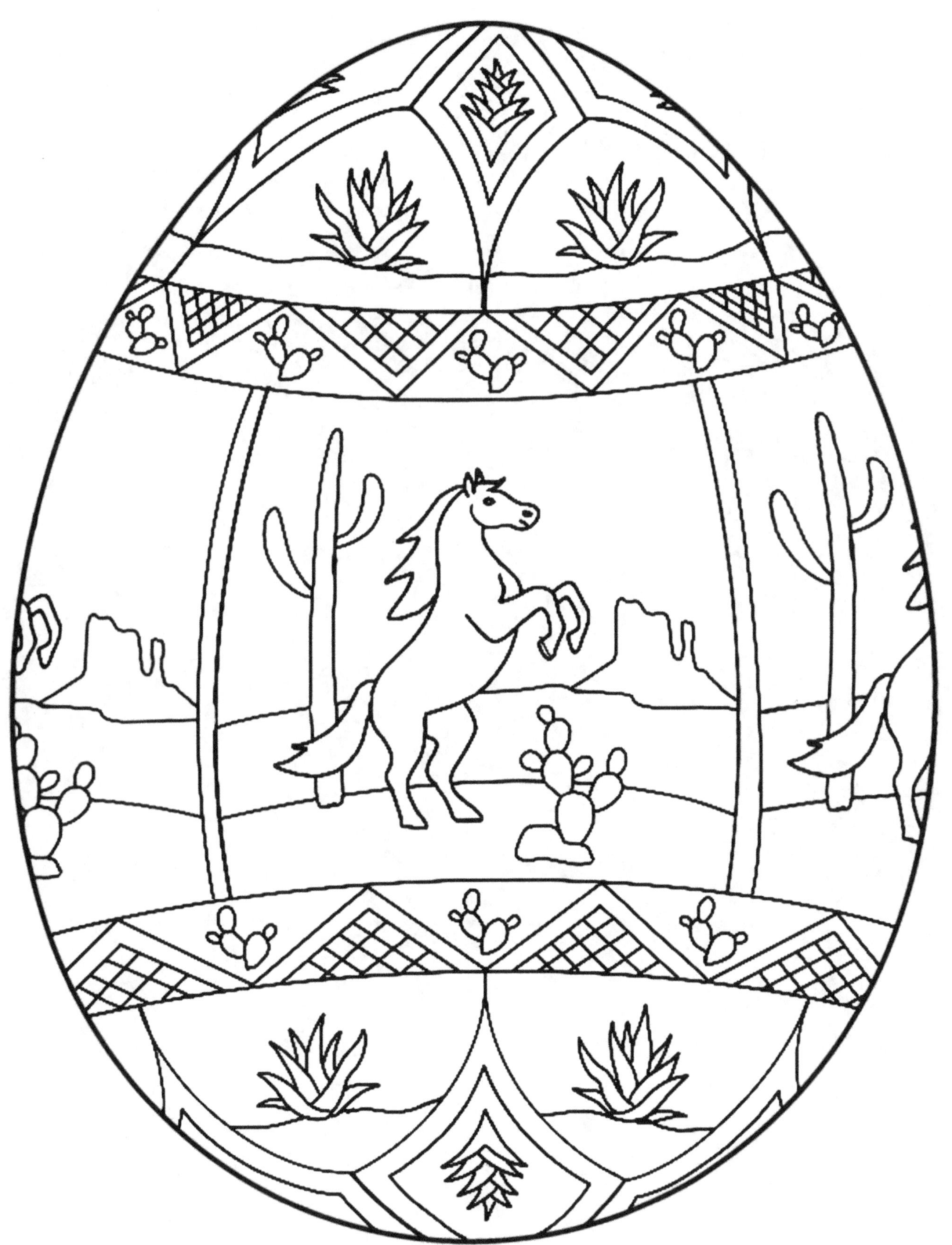

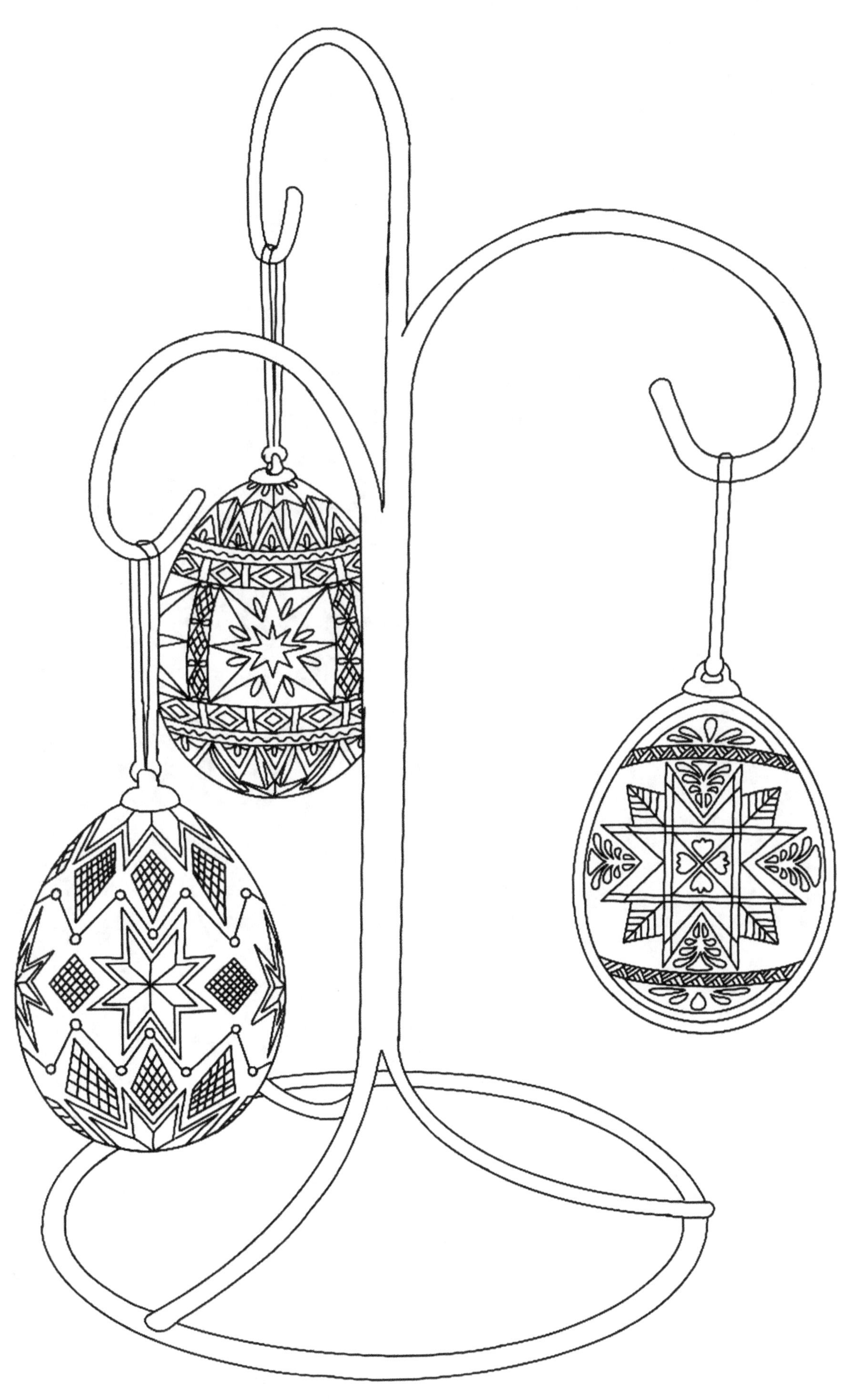

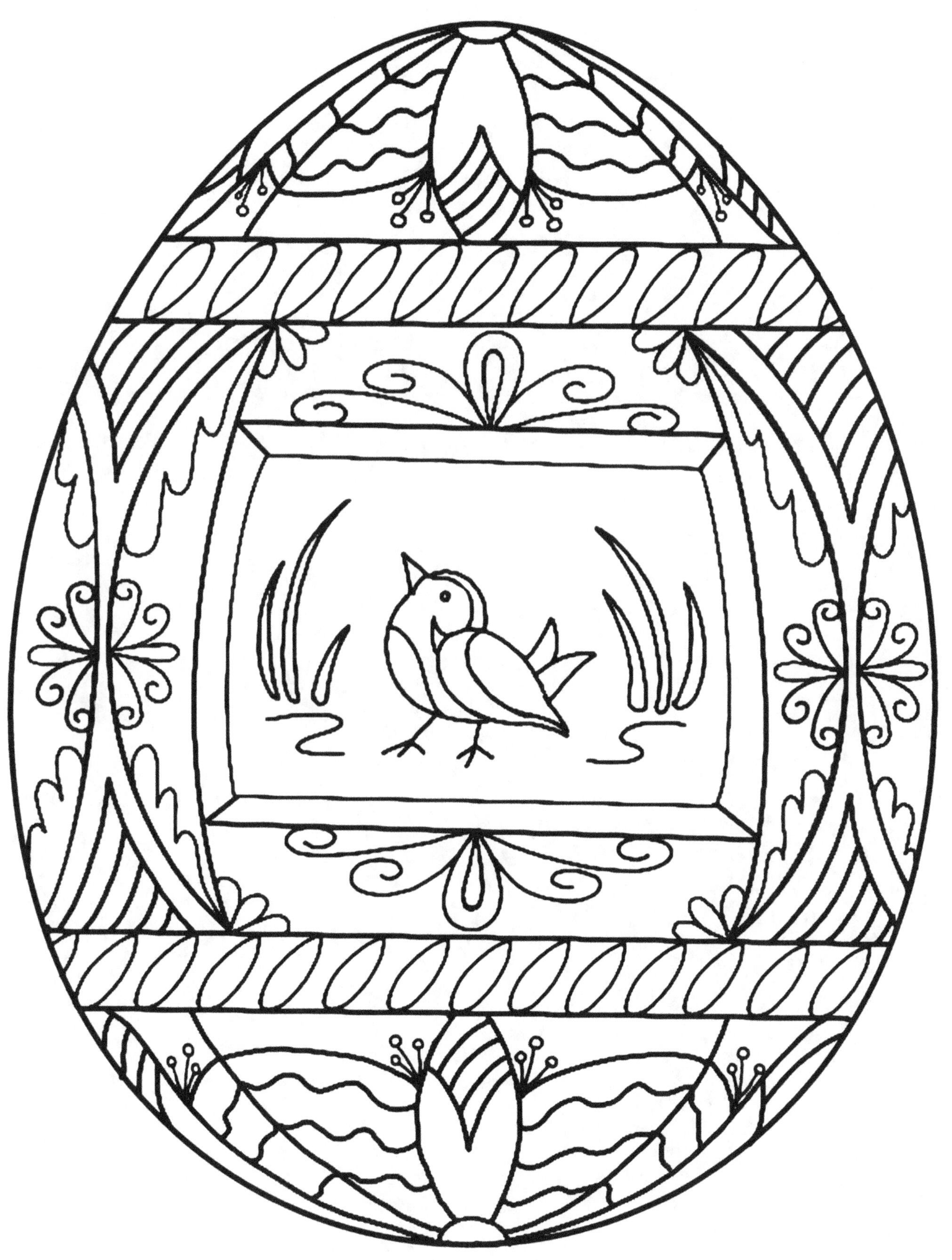

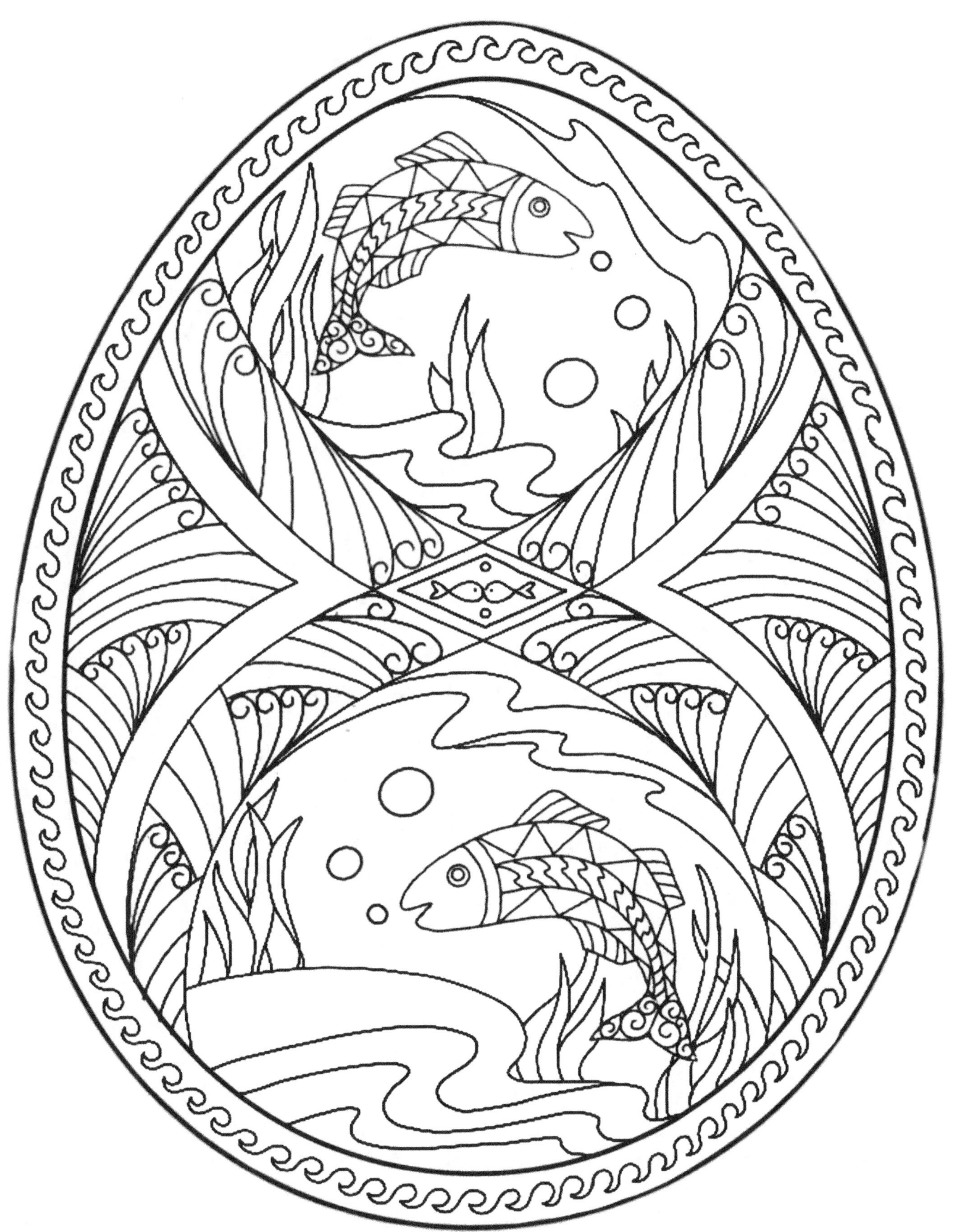

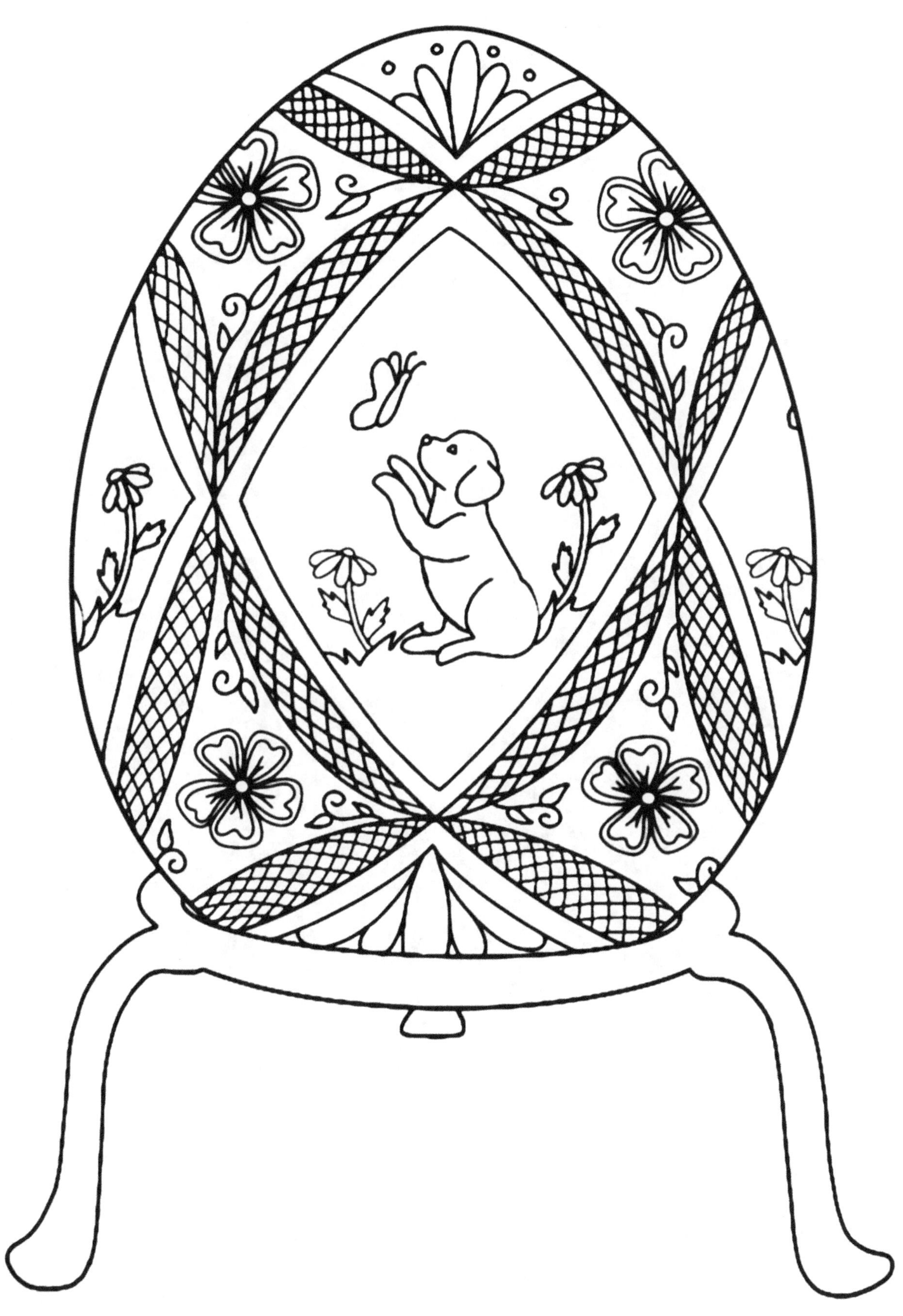

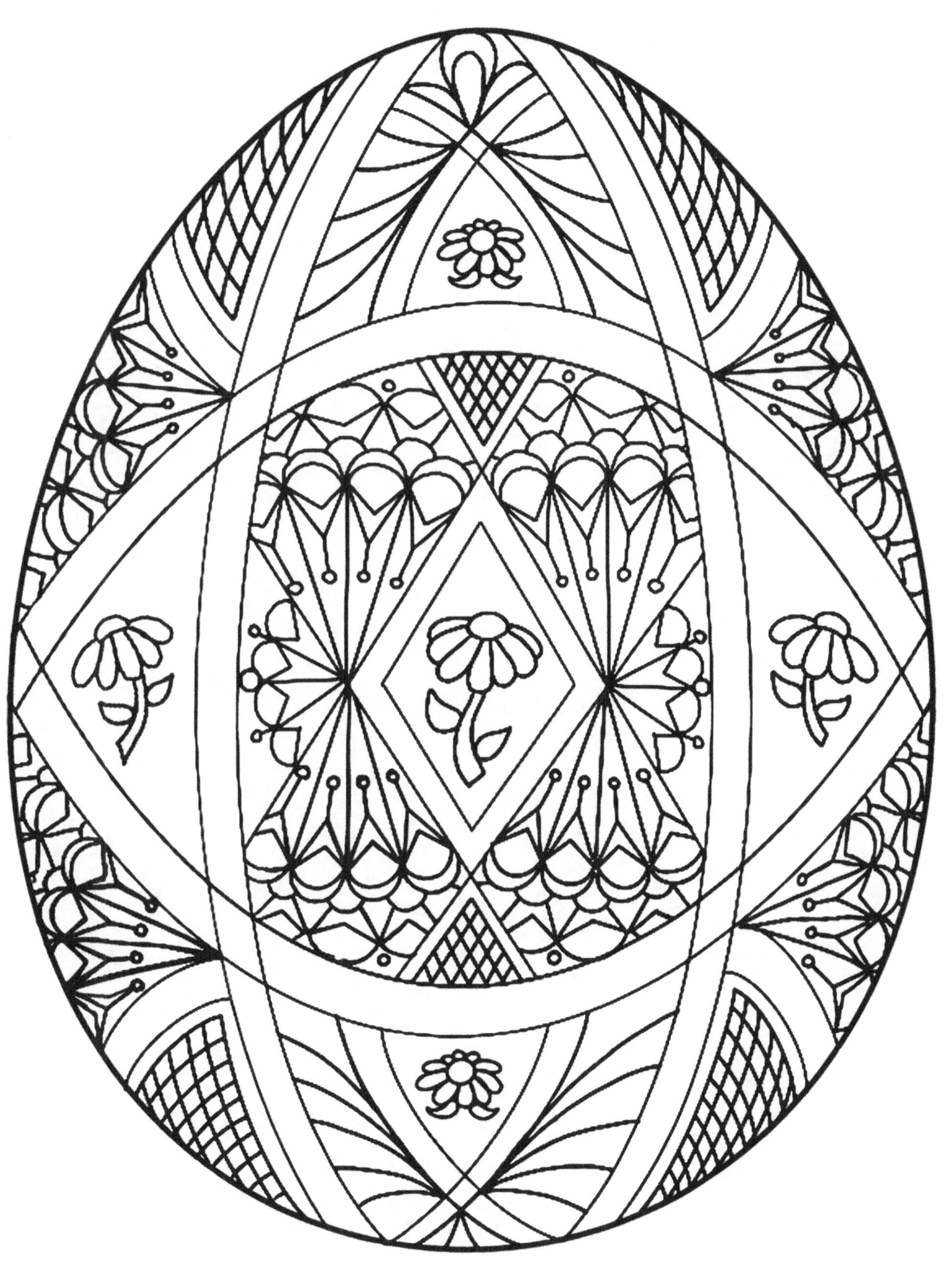

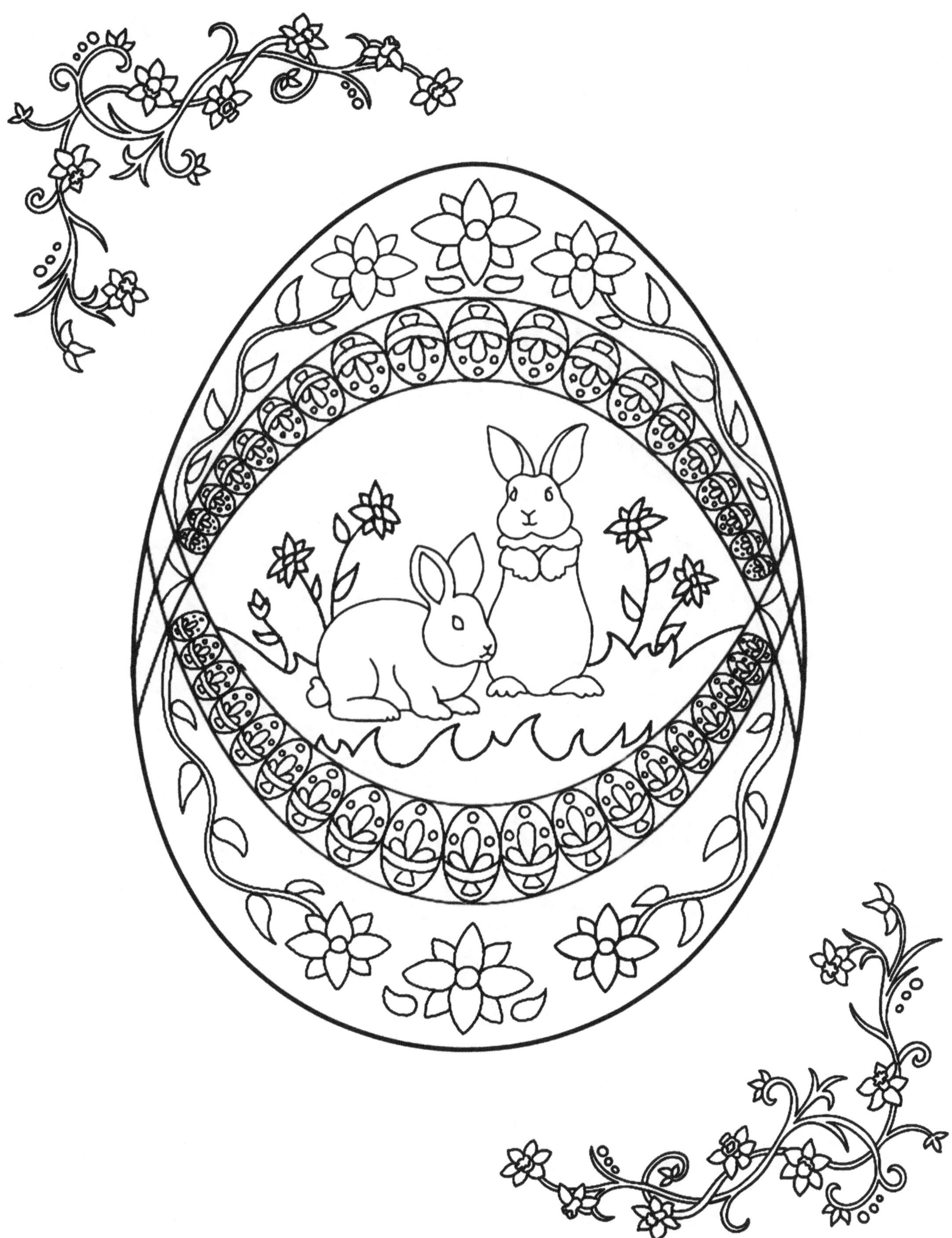

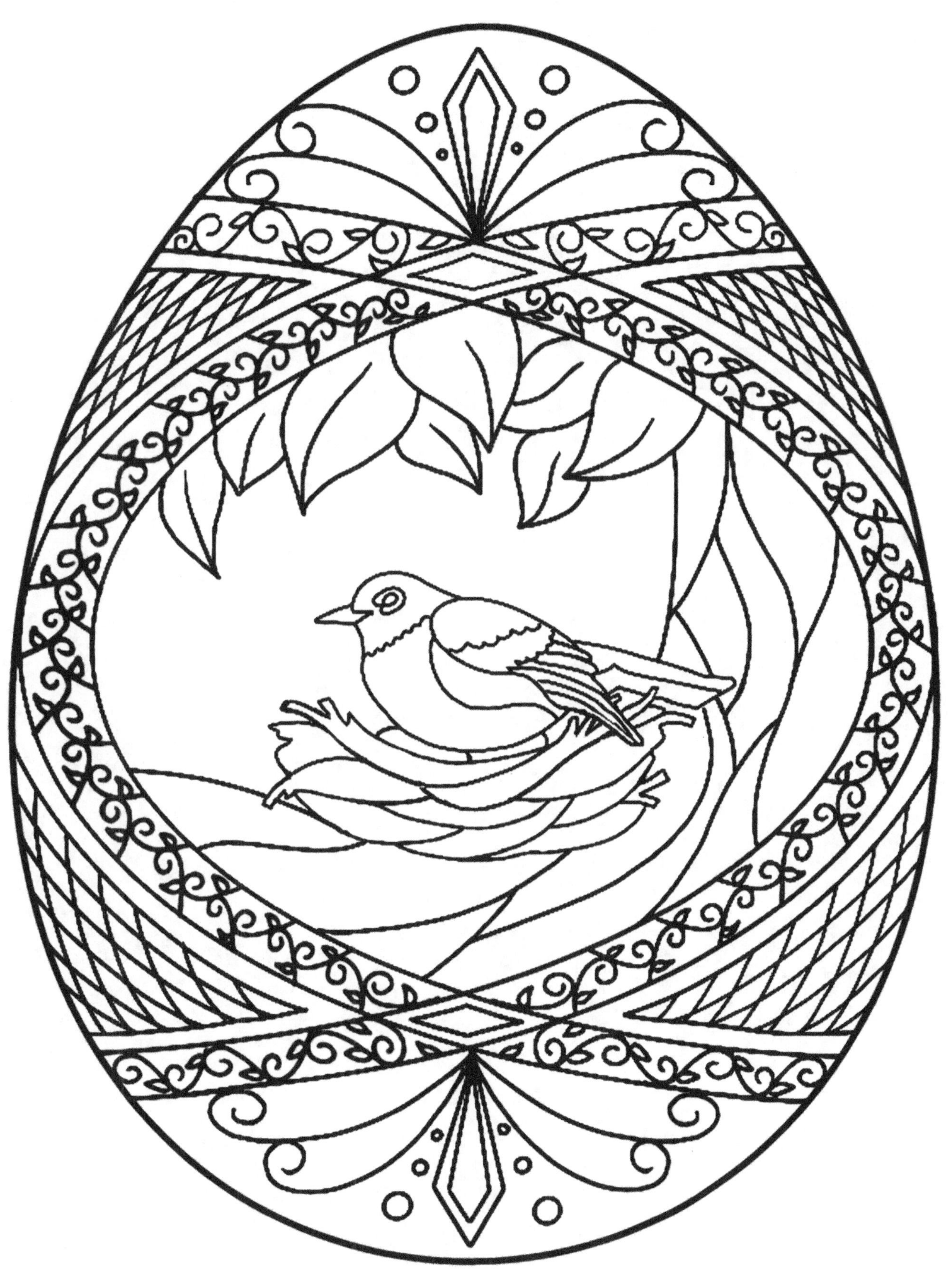

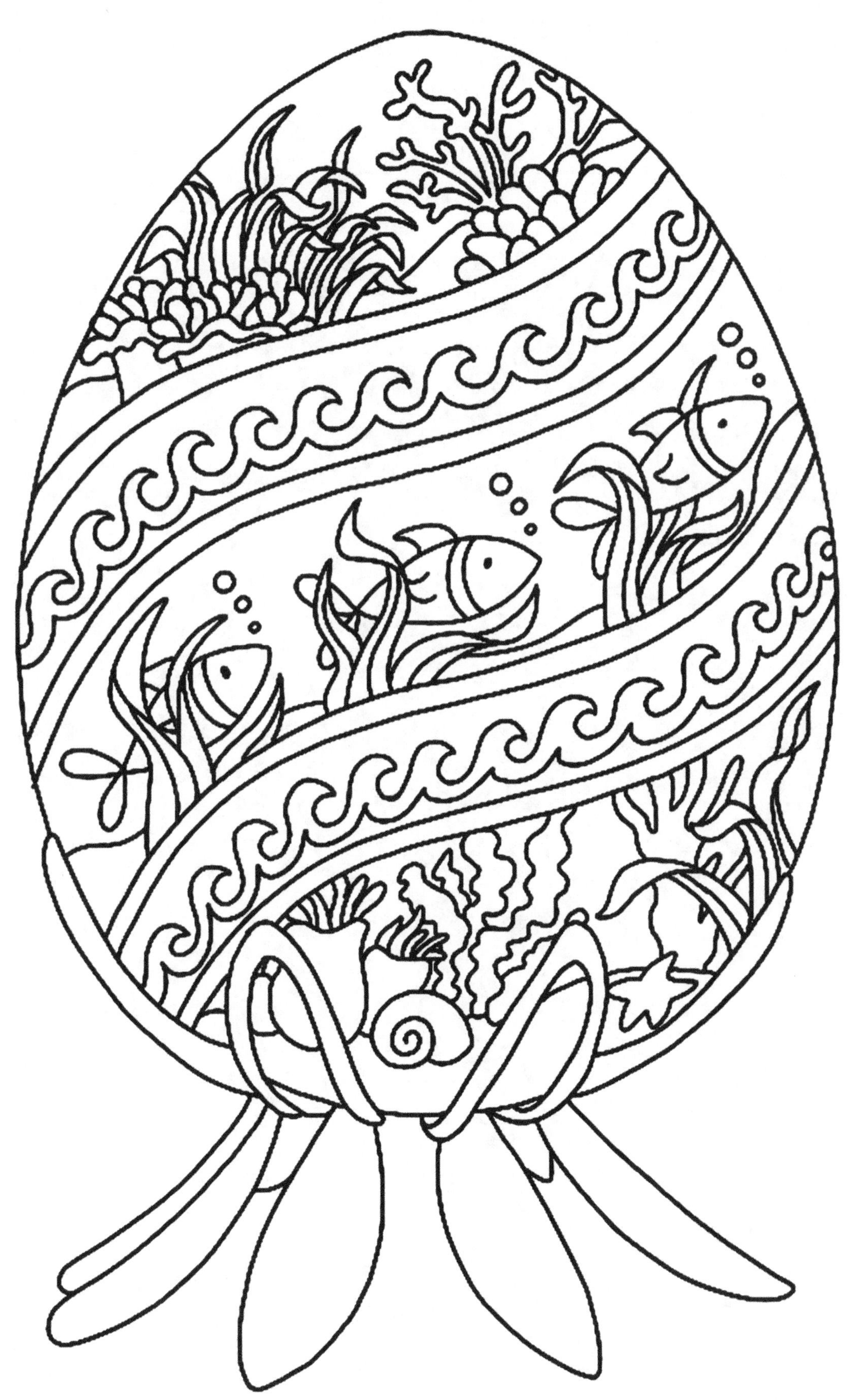

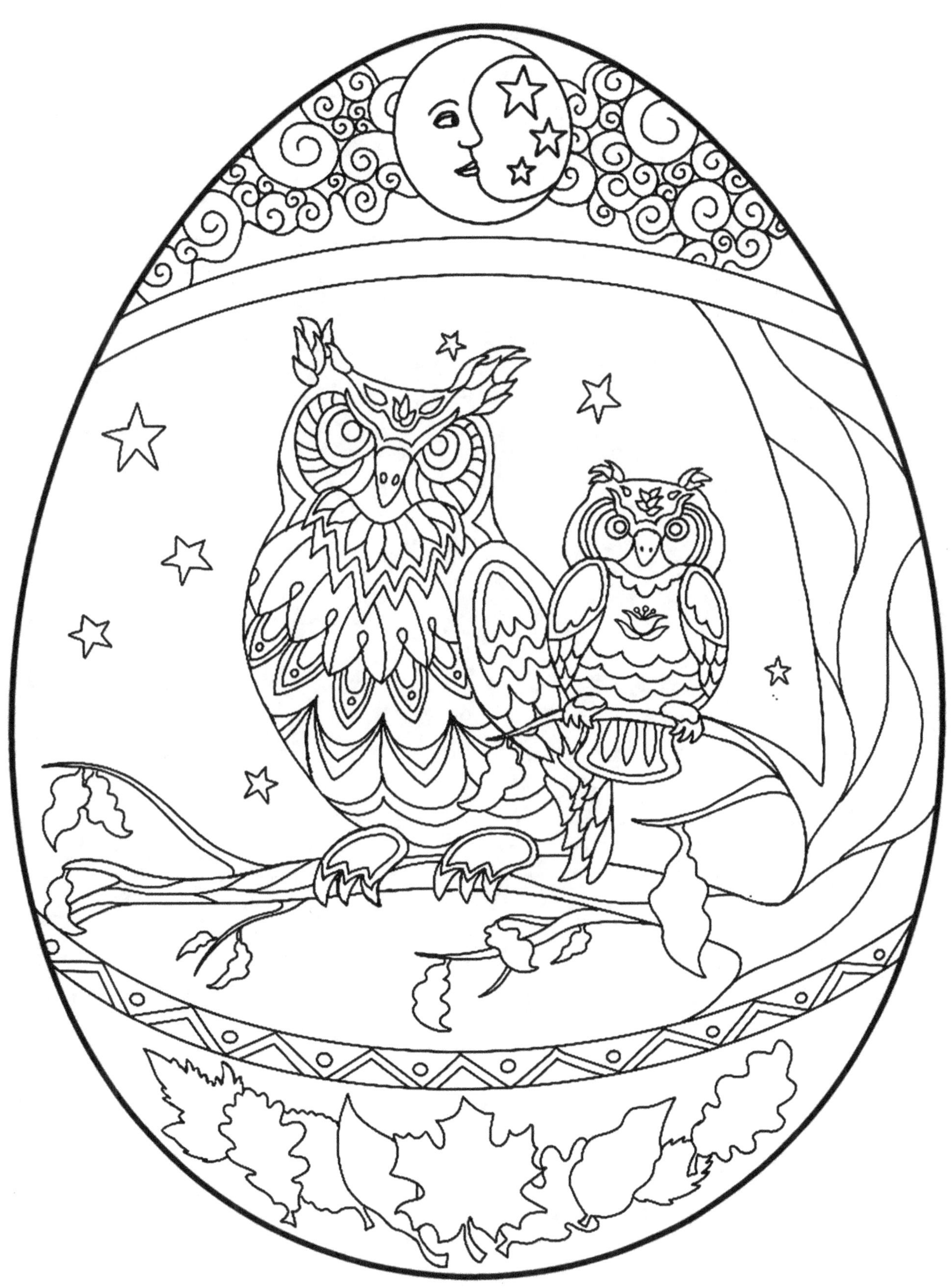

9 781732 262638